NEWTON PAGE

NEWTON PAGE

THE LIFE OF JOHN LAW

By

JOHN PHILIP WOOD

NEWTON PAGE

NEWTON PAGE

The Life of John Law

By

John Philip Wood

First published by Adam Black, North Ridge
and Longman & Co. London as

*'Memoirs of the Life of John Law of Lauriston
Including a Detailed Account of the Rise, Progress and
Termination of the Mississippi System'*

First published by Newton Page 2009

1 3 5 7 9 10 8 6 4 2

ISBN 978-1-934619-01-8
Library of Congress Control Number: 2009942925

Printed in the United States of America
Set in Adobe Garamond Pro

CONTENTS

THE LIFE OF JOHN LAW

THE LIFE OF JOHN LAW

John Law of Lauriston, Comptroller General of the Finances of France, one of the most remarkable characters of modern times, was born in the capital of Scotland in April 1671, his baptism being thus entered in the Registers of Edinburgh on the 21st of that month, 'William Law, goldsmith, and Jean Campbell, a son named John. Witnesses, Mr. John Law, John Law, goldsmith, Archibald Hislop, bookbinder, Heugh Campbell, John Melvill, and John Murray, merchants.'

His father, William Law, according to communications made by an agent of the family, was great-grandson of James Law, Archbishop of Glasgow from 1615 to 1632, and second son of James Law of Brunton in Fife, by Margaret, daughter of Sir John Preston of Prestonhall, Baronet. He followed the profession of a goldsmith in Edinburgh, a business, at that time, partaking more of the nature of a banker's than of that to which the name is now restricted, with such success as enabled him to purchase the lands of Lauriston and Randleston. This property, extending to upwards of 180 Scottish acres, stretching along the south shore of the Firth of Forth, in the parish of Cramond and county of Edinburgh, was acquired by him from Margaret Dalgliesh, only child and heiress of Robert Dalgliesh of Lauriston, relict of Lewis Craig of Riccartoun, with consent of Thomas Craig of Riccartoun, her eldest son, by disposition dated 14th June, 1683. In that disposition, the right to these lands is taken to William Law and Jean Campbell, his wife, and the longest liver of the two in liferent, and to John Law, their eldest son, in fee; and a charter under the great seal to that effect was granted 20th July, 1683.[1] It appears that William Law did not long survive this purchase, as on the 25th of September, 1684, John Law was served heir of William Law, goldsmith, burgess of Edinburgh, his father.[2] Jean Campbell, his wife, descended from one of the numerous branches of the ducal house of Argyll, survived him many years, and by her prudent management, preserved the estate of Lauriston to the family.

John Law of Lauriston, their eldest surviving son, was educated at Edinburgh, and made a competent progress in literature. The bent of his inclination, however, prompting him to apply, in a particular manner, to the studies of arithmetic and geometry, he made himself so complete a master of these branches as to be able to resolve with the utmost facility the most intricate problems in them; and it was remarked that none more perfectly understood the complex science of algebra. He likewise bestowed much time and labour to acquire a deep insight into the principles of public and private credit; the state of trade and manufactures; the theory and practice of taxation; and, in short, of all circumstances respecting political economy in general. The accession of knowledge, resulting from these inquiries, laid the foundation of his future eminence.[3]

He lost his father before he had completed his 14th year, experiencing the disadvantages of emancipation from paternal control at an early age. The graces of a naturally handsome

1. Mag. Sig, Ixix. 58.

2. Inq. Ret. xxxix. 502.

3. Histoire du Systême des Finances, i. 68. Mémoires de Pollnitz, ii. 245.

person were carefully improved by the acquisition of external accomplishments. For these, indeed, he became so remarkable, as to be known among his companions by the name of Jessamy John; and he was commonly distinguished by the appellation of Beau Law. He addicted himself to the practice of all games of chance, skill, and dexterity, and was noted as a capital player at tennis, an exercise much in vogue in Scotland towards the close of the seventeenth century.[4]

The usual result of neglecting honest and lawful pursuits, and wasting time and talents in idleness, gambling, and dissipation, followed. Mr. Law went to London, and involved himself so deeply, that he found it necessary to dispose of the fee of Lauriston, which, as already stated, was vested in him. This he conveyed to his mother, Jean Campbell, by disposition dated at London 6th February, 1692. Mrs. Law undertook the payment of his debts, advanced money to him, and by her industry and good management, relieved the estate of Lauriston of every burden; after which, she executed entails to continue that property in the family.

In London, Mr. Law's superior personal beauty, ready wit, and engaging manners, aided by his propensity to deep play, procured him admittance into some of the first circles. He had the reputation of being extremely fortunate in affairs of gallantry. One of these was attended with disastrous consequences. A Mrs. Lawrence was the occasion of a quarrel between him and Mr. Edward Wilson, fifth son of Thomas Wilson of Keythorpe, in the county of Leicester, which led to a hostile meeting between the parties in Bloomsbury Square, 9th April, 1694, when Mr. Wilson was killed on the spot.

Mr. Law was immediately apprehended, and was brought

4. Information from the late Sir David Dalrymple, Lord Hailes. Transactions of the Society of Antiquaries of Scotland, i. 503.

to trial before the King and Queen's Commissioners, who sat at the Justice Hall in the Old Bailey, on the 18th, 19th, and 20th of April, 1694. In the proceedings published by authority, the statement is thus given: John Law, of St. Giles's in the Fields, gentleman, was arraigned upon an indictment for murder, for killing Edward Wilson, gentleman, commonly called Beau Wilson, a person who, by the common report of fame, kept a coach and six horses maintained his family in great splendour and grandeur, being full of money, no one complaining of his being their debtor, yet from whence he had the effects which caused him to appear in so great an equipage, is hard to be determined. The matter of fact was this, some difference happened to arise between Mr. Law and the deceased concerning a Mrs. Lawrence, who was acquainted with Mr. Law; upon which, on the 9th of April instant, they met in Bloomsbury Square, and there fought a duel, in which Mr. Wilson was killed. It was made appear also that they had met several times before, but had not opportunity to fight; besides, there were several letters sent by Mr. Law, or given to Mr. Wilson by him, which letters were full of invectives and cautions to Mr. Wilson to beware, for there was a design of evil against him; and there were two letters sent by Mr. Wilson, one to Mr. Law and the other to Mrs. Lawrence. Mr. Wilson's man, Smith, swore that Mr. Law came to his master's house, a little before the fatal meeting, and drank a pint of sack in the parlour; after which, he heard his master say that he was much surprised with something that Mr. Law had told him. Captain Wightman, a person of good information, gave an account of the whole matter. He said that he was a familiar friend of Mr. Wilson, was with him and Mr. Law at the Fountain Tavern in the Strand, and after they had stayed a little while there Mr. Law went away. After this, Mr. Wilson and Captain Wightman took coach and were driven towards Bloomsbury, where Mr.

Wilson stepped out of the coach into the square, where Mr. Law met him; and before they came together Mr. Wilson drew his sword and stood upon his guard. Upon which, Mr. Law immediately drew his sword; and they both passed together, making but one pass, by which Mr. Wilson received a mortal wound in the upper part of the stomach, of the depth of two inches, of which he instantly died. The letters read in court were full of aggravations on both parts, without any name subscribed to them. There were other witnesses that saw the duel fought, who all agreed in their depositions that they drew their swords, and passed at each other, and presently Mr. Wilson was killed. This was the sum of the evidence for the Crown.

Mr. Law, in his defence, declared that Mr. Wilson and he had been together several times before the duel was fought, and no quarrel ever took place between them till they met at the Fountain Tavern, which was occasioned about the letters; and that his meeting with Mr. Wilson in Bloomsbury was merely an accidental thing, Mr. Wilson drawing his sword upon him first, by which he was forced to stand in his own defence: that the misfortune did arise only from a sudden heat of passion, and not from any malice prepense. The Court acquainted the Jury, that if they found Mr. Law and Mr. Wilson did make an agreement to fight, though Mr. Wilson drew first; that Mr. Law killed him, he was, by the construction of the law, guilty of murder; for if two men suddenly quarrel, and one kill the other, this would be but manslaughter; but this case seems to be otherwise, for there was a continual quarrel carried on between them for some time before; therefore, must be accounted a malicious quarrel, and a design of murder in the person that killed the other. The trial lasted long, and the prisoner had persons of good quality who gave a fair account of his life in general, and that he was not given to quarrelling, nor a person of ill behaviour. The Jury having considered of a verdict very seriously, found that Mr.

Law was guilty of murder, and sentence of death was passed on him, 20th April, 1694.[5]

On a representation of the case to the crown Mr. Law obtained a pardon, but an appeal being lodged by a brother of the deceased, he was detained in the King's Bench Prison. This appeal was brought before the Court of King's Bench in Trinity Term, 1694; several exceptions were taken on the part of Mr. Law, which were overruled.[6] While this was depending, Mr. Law found means to make his escape from confinement; on which occasion the following advertisement was published in the London Gazette of Monday, 7th January, 1695:—'Captain[7] John Lawe, a Scotchman, lately a prisoner in the King's Bench for murder, aged 26, a very tall, black, lean man, well shaped, above six foot high, large pockholes in his face, big high nosed, speaks broad and loud, made his escape from the said prison. Whoever secures him, so as he may be delivered at the said prison, shall have fifty pounds paid immediately by the Marshall of the King's Bench.' This advertisement proved ineffectual, Mr. Law getting clear off, and it was probably at this time that he first visited the continent. The description, indeed, conveying no favourable idea of his personal appearance, and differing

---

5. Nichols' History and Antiquities of the County of Leicester, iii. 487, where it is stated that Mr. Edward Wilson was the wonder of the age he lived in, as, from the moderate fortune of a country gentleman's younger son, he was on a sudden exalted to a very high pitch. For gay dress, splendid equipage, and vast expense, he exceeded all the Court. How he was supported, few, very few indeed, truly knew; and those who have undertaken to account for it, have done it only from the darkness and uncertainty of conjecture.

6. See Salkeld's Reports, i. 59, voce Appeal.

7. It does not appear that he had the honour of bearing any military commission. Captain is a good travelling title, and it is said that he served some time as an officer of the Walloon Guards in Spain.

from his real portrait, seems to have been drawn up with a view to facilitate his escape, which, it is reported, was effected by the proper application of money; and it is to be observed that he was then in the 24th, not the 26th year of his age.

Mr. Law appears to have made good use of the period of his exile, improving his knowledge of finance by observing the various modes of conducting the banking establishments, managing the public revenues, and the state of trade and manufactures in the different countries that he passed through; particularly by making himself as much as possible acquainted, upon the spot, with the operations of the mysterious bank of Amsterdam, which, it is stated, he was the better enabled to do, from officiating for some time as secretary to the British resident in Holland. He returned to his native country towards the close of the seventeenth century; the introduction to his *Proposals and Reasons for Constituting a Council of Trade*, being dated at Edinburgh, 31st December, 1700; and the work was published there early in the ensuing year.

In this work he submits to the public a plan for reviving, encouraging, and promoting the trade and manufactures of the kingdom—then, in consequence of various unfortunate circumstances, particularly the miscarriage of the Darien expedition, at a very low ebb by constituting, by an act of Parliament, a Council of Trade, in whom should be vested the whole of the king's revenues, the Bishop's lands and rents, all charitable endowments and appropriations, one-tenth of all grain raised, and malt made in the kingdom, one-twentieth of all sums sued for at law, one-fortieth of all successions, legacies, and sales, and several other articles. This great income he proposed to employ, after deduction of a fixed annual sum for his Majesty's use, and for the salaries of the members of the council, in promoting, by all manner of ways, the trade, fisheries, and manufactures of Scotland, building workhouses, and purchasing all means and materials for employing, relieving, and maintaining the poor, buying up, and keeping at a regular rate, the various productions and manufactures of the kingdom, making and maintaining highways, bridges, and harbours, and in other beneficial purposes. He also proposes that the council should be empowered to dispense with prejudicial monopolies, regulate the weights and measures, punish fraudulent bankrupts, liberate honest debtors who have made a fair surrender of their effects, and seize upon all beggars and vagabonds; and it is further submitted, that all duties upon exports, and upon such imports as are proper to be meliorated or manufactured in the kingdom, should be taken off, one percent only excepted, but that the duties on all other imports should be doubled.

From the exertions of a Council vested with such powers, and possessing revenues so ample, Mr. Law entertained the most sanguine expectations of a speedy recovery of the trade and manufactures of Scotland, from the depressed state in which, at that time, they were; but the project did not appear in the same light to the supreme judicature of the kingdom, during the reign of King William; and, consequently, met with no encouragement.

This publication had, however, the effect of introducing Mr. Law to the notice of several of the principal personages of this country; and he soon became intimate with the first Duke of Argyll, his sons the Marquis of Lorn and Lord Archibald Campbell, the Marquis of Tweeddale, and other noblemen. Relying on their powerful support, he, in 1705, offered to Parliament a plan for removing the difficulties Scotland then lay under, from the great scarcity of specie, and the stoppage of payments of the bank; preparatory to and explanatory of which, he published another work, entitled *Money and Trade Considered, With a Proposal for Supplying the Nation with*

Money, printed at Edinburgh the same year.

After preliminary observations tending to show the insufficiency of gold and silver to serve as money, from their increasing in quantity as the demand lessens, and the superiority of land as a foundation for money, being capable of improvement as the demand increases, and the quantity remaining always the same, he therein proposes that commissioners, to be appointed by, and to act under the control of Parliament, should have power to issue notes, and to give them out in any of these three modes, (i) in the way of loan, at ordinary interest, upon landed security, the debt not to exceed half or two-thirds of the value of the land; (ii) to give out the full price of land in notes, and to enter into the possession thereof by wadset, redeemable within a certain period; and (iii) to give out in notes the full price of land upon sale irredeemably. Thus, all the notes being firmly secured on landed property, he asserts that they will not only be equal in value to gold and silver money of the same denomination, but also be preferred to these metals, as not being liable to fall in value like them.

This scheme, although supported by the united weight of the court party, and of that called the *Squadrone*, (a few monied men excepted,) beaded by the Duke of Argyll, and the Marquis of Tweeddale, was rejected by Parliament, the House passing a resolution, 'that to establish any kind of paper credit, so as to oblige it to pass, was an improper expedient for the nation.' The rejection of this plan was occasioned by an apprehension that if it took effect, all the estates in the kingdom would thereby be brought to a complete dependence upon the government.[8]

Mr. Law now resolved to abandon his native country, and try his fortune abroad.[9] He resided some time at Brussels, where he

8. Lockhart of Carnwath's Memoirs, 144, 145.

9. It is said that Mr. Law was employed in settling the proportion of the equivalent to be paid by England to Scotland, on account of the

became noted for extraordinary success at play, to which his skill in calculation did not a little contribute. In two excursions he made to Paris, his good fortune became still more conspicuous; Pharaoh was his favourite, and at this game he was accustomed to play at the Hotel de Gesvres, Rue des Poulies, at the houses of Poisson, Rue Dauphine, and of Duclos, a famous comedian, which were his ordinary haunts, although his company was greatly sought after by persons of the first rank. It is said that he seldom carried with him less than 100,000 livres in gold, every time he went to these places, where the play at last became so deep, that Mr. Law, finding it was with difficulty his hands could contain the sums to be collected from and distributed among the gamesters at the end of every deal, was obliged to provide himself with counters, rated at 18 louis each, in order to facilitate his operations.

Visiting the principal cities of Italy, he continued his speculations, playing at all sorts of games, betting, and engaging in the public funds and banks, with his usual success, particularly at Rome in time of the carnival, at Venice and Genoa, insomuch that in 1714 he was worth upwards of £10,000 sterling.[10] It is said that his good fortune at play giving umbrage to some people at Paris, who could not bear to see a foreigner so successful, they found means to have him represented in the light of a state enemy, to M. d'Argenson,

union of the two kingdoms. The authority for this assertion is however questionable, and it appears that he was at Genoa so early as 1708.

10. Mr. Law, in his memorial to the Duc de Bourbon, of 15th October, 1724, to be afterwards noticed, says he brought into France in 1714, 1,000,000 livres, at 28 livres to the marc. It would appear that he had improved his circumstances previously to going abroad, as, among the burdens on the estate of Pitreavie, in Fife, sold in 1711 by the Earl of Rosebery to Sir Robert Blackwood, was an annuity of £1455 Scots to John Law of Lauriston.

Lieutenant-General of the Police, who sent orders to Mr. Law to leave Paris within twenty-four hours; and that he found himself in a similar predicament at Genoa and Turin. After leaving the latter city, he passed some time in travelling through Germany and Hungary, in his accustomed style of play and expense.[11]

Much as Mr. Law was addicted to gambling, he did not, however, suffer that passion to gain a complete ascendancy over his mind. Conscious of his abilities, and sensible of the depth of his knowledge in the art of finance, he ardently longed for an opportunity of bringing both into action. Accordingly, on his first visit to Paris, he found means to procure an introduction to the Duc de Chartres, afterwards Duc d'Orléans, and Regent of France, with whom, as also with Chamillard, the then Comptroller-General, he held several conferences concerning the possibility of reducing the national debt. On Mr. Law's coming to Paris for the second time, the Abbé Thesul recommended him to Desmarets, successor to Chamillard in the office of Comptroller-General, to whom he communicated a plan for remedying the disorders of the finances, but this it was not thought proper to adopt. It is stated, that this plan being laid by Desmarets before Louis XIV the bigotry of that monarch led him, instead of inquiring into the merits of the project, to ask whether the proposer was a catholic; and, on being answered in the negative, to say that he would have nothing to do with a heretic.[12]

During these various rambles, Mr. Law, by means of his graceful figure and insinuating manners, was everywhere well received by persons of the highest quality, sovereign princes themselves taking pleasure in his company and conversation. At

11. Hist. Syst. i. 70, 71. Oeuvres de J. Law, 430.

12. Mémoires de la Minorité de Louis XV par Massillon, 99. Fragmens des Lettres Originates de Madame Charlotte Elizabeth de Baviere, Veuve de Monsieur, frere unique de Louis XIV. ii. 271.

Florence he became very intimate with the Prince de Vendôme, at that time Grand Prior of France, who did not scruple to ask the loan of a very considerable sum, which Mr. Law lent him with the best grace in the world. Becoming acquainted at Neufchatel, with the Prince of Conti, he imparted some of his financial projects to his Highness, who thought so favourably of them as to write on the subject to the Duke of Burgundy, grandson of Louis XIV. To Victor Amadeus, King of Sardinia, by whom he was particularly noticed, Mr. Law communicated a scheme of the same nature as that which was afterwards proposed to the Duc d'Orléans; but that monarch declined putting it in practice, saying that his dominions were too small for the execution of so great a design; at the same time mentioning that France was the proper theatre for its performance. If I know the disposition of the people of that kingdom, added he, I am sure they will relish your schemes; and, therefore, I would advise you to go thither.[13]

Adopting this sound advice, Mr. Law visited Paris for the third time in 1714, not long before Louis XIV gave way to fate, bringing with him the whole of his acquisitions during his various rambles and adventures, and fixing his residence in the Place Vendôme, or de Louis le Grand. After the demise of that monarch, his old friend the Duc d'Orléans, assuming the government of the kingdom as regent during the minority of Louis XV. Mr. Law renewed his acquaintance with that prince, who being fond of men of spirit, vivacity and wit, could not fail of being highly delighted with that enterprising foreigner, as he not only possessed these qualities in an eminent degree, but was, besides, of a disposition not less addicted to pleasure and dissipation than his own. Mr. Law consequently rose to no small degree of favour and intimacy with his Royal Highness, who soon finding the extent of his capacity, and

13. Massillon, 100. Pollnitz, ii. 237.

the fertility of his resources, admitted him into all his private parties, and nominated him one of the Counsellors of State. Availing himself of that intimacy, Mr. Law took care not to neglect every opportunity in his power to draw the attention of the regent to the state of the French finances, at that time in a situation accounted desperate by all who pretended to skill in these affairs, the long and expensive wars of Louis XIV having superinduced an enormous weight of debt upon the nation, which groaned under the intolerable load of taxes imposed for payment of the interest. All industry was thus checked; trade in a manner annihilated; manufactures, commerce, and navigation had almost ceased; the merchant and the trader were reduced to beggary, and the artificer was compelled, for want of employment, to leave the kingdom. In short, such was the state of affairs, that it had been debated in council, and proposed to the regent, to expunge at once the debts of the state by a national bankruptcy. This proposal he nobly rejected, preferring to it the more equitable method of establishing a commission or *Visa*, to inquire into the claims of the state creditors. By this commission the national debt was at last put into a kind of order, and the amount reduced to somewhat more than 2000 millions of livres, which, at 28 livres to the marc of standard silver, (two pounds sterling,) the then denomination of the specie in France, made above 142 millions sterling. Of this sum, 1750 millions of livres were established upon particular funds, at the rate of four percent; and for the remaining 250 millions, the creditors obtained *billets d'état*, as they were called, bearing also an interest of four percent; making altogether 80 millions of interest per annum, which, from the distressed situation of the kingdom, was very irregularly paid; and after doing that, there hardly remained, out of an ill-collected revenue, a sum sufficient to defray the necessary expense of the civil government.[14]

This calamitous situation of affairs, which would have daunted a man of less spirit and enterprise, had no other effect than to render Mr. Law more eager to provide some remedy for these evils. The most efficacious mode he judged to be the establishment of a well regulated paper credit; but as this matter was, little understood, if not altogether unknown, in France, he thought proper, in order to pave the way for its introduction, to translate into French his publication on Money and Trade, and to explain its principles in a series of letters, addressed to the Duc d'Orléans, and in two memorials presented to that prince. In these he strongly inculcates his favourite maxim, that the power and prosperity of a state increases in proportion to the quantity of money circulating therein; and after asserting that even the richest nations have not specie sufficient to afford full employment to all their inhabitants, and to carry their trade to the height of which it is capable, he launches out into encomiums on the advantages of paper credit for supplying that defect. In support of this proposition, he instances the vast benefits accruing to England and to Holland, from the banks of London and Amsterdam; and adduces a variety of arguments to show that the setting up of an establishment of a similar nature, but upon an improved plan, in Paris, would be attended with the like good effects to France.[15]

Hoping that by these arguments the regent was convinced of the utility and necessity of such an establishment, Mr. Law proposed to set up a bank, secured upon landed property unalienably engaged, and upon the whole royal revenues, to be administered in the king's name, but subject to the control of Commissioners appointed by the States General of the kingdom;

14. Duclos, i. 354. Stewart's Inquiry into the Principles of Political Economy, ii. 236.

15. Oeuvres de J. Law, passim.

blending in this scheme the two plans for establishing a Council of Trade in Scotland, and supplying that nation with money, formerly mentioned. This application was, however, ineffectual at that time, as we learn from the preamble of his Majesty's letters patent of 2nd May, 1716, where it is said, that 'Mr. Law having some time since proposed a scheme for erecting a bank, which should consist of our own money, and be administered in our name, and under our authority, the project was examined in our Council of Finances, where several bankers, merchants, and deputies from our trading cities being convened, and required to give their advice, they were unanimous in the opinion, that nothing could be more advantageous to our kingdom, which, through its situation and fertility, added to the industry of its inhabitants, stood in need of nothing more than a solid credit, for acquiring the most extensive and flourishing commerce. They thought, however, that the present conjuncture was not favourable for the undertaking; and this reason, added to some particular clauses of the project, determined us to refuse it.'[16]

Not discouraged by this repulse, Mr. Law requested permission to set up a private bank in his house, in the Place de Louis le Grand, to be composed entirely of funds furnished by himself and by those who chose to engage in the undertaking, proposing, by means thereof, to increase the circulation of money; put a stop to the progress of usury; facilitate the exchange between Paris and the Provinces; augment the consumption of manufactures; and enable the people the more easily to pay the heavy taxes to which they were subjected. This bank was accordingly established by letters patent, bearing date the 2nd and 20th of May, 1716, containing the following regulations.

The stock of the bank to consist of 1200 actions, or shares, of 1000 crowns, or 5000 livres each, the denomination being then fixed by law at forty livres the marc, consequently,

16. Mémoires de la Régence de S. A. R. Mgr. le Duc d'Orléans, i. 133.

each share was worth £250, and the whole stock £300,000 sterling. All persons whatsoever to be at liberty to subscribe for as many shares as they pleased, and it was declared that the bank securities belonging to, as well as the money lodged in it by, foreigners, should not be subject to any confiscation or attachment whatsoever, even in case of war with the nations to which the proprietors respectively belonged. All questions to be determined by plurality of votes, those possessing from five to ten to have one vote; from ten to fifteen shares to have two votes, and so on in proportion; but those who had less than five shares were to be excluded from any voice in the management. The accounts to be balanced twice per year, *viz* from the 15th to the 20th of June, and from the 15th to the 20th of January. Two general courts to be held yearly, in which, the state of the company's affairs should be discussed, and the dividends settled. The treasurer never to have more than 200,000 crowns, nor any of the cashiers more than 20,000 in hand at a time; and they were besides obliged to find sufficient security for their intromissions. The notes to be signed by the director, and by one of the proprietors, and to be revised by an inspector appointed by the regent. The bank not to undertake any sort of commerce whatever, nor to charge itself with the execution of any commissions; the notes to be all payable at sight, and no money allowed to be borrowed by the bank on any pretext whatever. Various regulations were added of less importance, and too long to be enumerated in this place.

This association, of which, Mr. Law and his brother William, then settled at London, were the principal partners, assumed the firm of the General Bank of Law and Company, and set out under very favourable auspices, it being known that they enjoyed the protection of the regent, and a high idea of their solidity being raised by the discourse Mr. Law unceasingly held in public, that a banker merited the punishment of death if he issued notes or bills of exchange without having their effective value in his repositories. But what most attracted the public confidence was, the security their notes provided against the arbitrary practice of varying the standard of the coin at the will of the monarch; an unjustifiable measure, frequently put in execution by the French government, to the infinite prejudice of debtors and creditors, particularly at the general coinages in 1709 and 1716, by the former of which the king gained twenty-three and one-thirteenth percent, and by the latter 20 percent, upon the whole specie of the kingdom. The terms in which the notes of the General Bank were couched, *viz* 'The bank promises to pay to the bearer, at sight, the sum of crowns, in coin of the weight and standard of this day,' (of the date of each note) 'value received,' effectually guarded against this contingency. Let us state, by way of example, that if one who had paid in, and taken out a bank note for, 1000 livres or 25 marcs, on the 2nd of June 1716, when the standard of the specie was settled by law at 40 livres per marc, wanted to exchange it at an after period, when the standard was fixed at 50 livres per marc, he would, on presenting his note, receive 25 marcs, or 1250 livres. The bank was, in like manner, secured from suffering if the reverse took place. On this account, as well as from the quickness and punctuality of the payments, and the orders given to the officers of the revenue in all parts in the kingdom to receive the paper, without discount, in payment of taxes, the notes of the General Bank in a short time rose to great repute, and were by many preferred to specie, insomuch that they soon came to pass current for one percent more than the coin itself. The most beneficial effects were thereby produced on the industry and trade of the nation, the taxes and royal revenues being, by means of the notes, remitted to the capital at little expense, and without draining the provinces of specie. Foreigners, who had hitherto been very cautious of dealing with the French, now began to interest themselves deeply in this new Bank; so that the balance of exchange with England and Holland soon rose to the rate of four and five percent in favour of Paris. This bank subsisted in high credit, to the no small profit of the proprietors,[17] till the close of the year 1718, when the Duc d'Orléans, observing the uncommon advantages resulting from that establishment, resolved to take it into his Majesty's hands, as at first proposed.[18]

This resolution, it may well be supposed, could not be relished by Mr. Law and his associates; but whatever were their sentiments, they knew the inutility of opposition to the will of the regent. They, however, endeavoured to obtain permission to continue the General Bank, at the same time the Royal Bank should be set on foot. This request was refused; and the public were informed, by act of council, bearing date 4th December, 1718, that the king had taken Mr. Law's bank into his own hands, under the name of the Royal Bank; that his Majesty had reimbursed the former proprietors their shares, and had become answerable for the outstanding notes issued by them, amounting to fifty-nine millions of livres. It was also declared, that no notes should, for the future, be fabricated, except in virtue of public acts of the king and council; and by a subsequent edict, his Majesty engaged that the notes should never be subjected to such diminutions as might be made on the specie, but that they should always be paid in full. Of this Royal Bank Mr.

17. At a general meeting of the proprietors, held in presence of the regent, 20th December 1717, it was determined to order a dividend of seven and one-half percent for six months, which is at the rate of fifteen percent per annum.

18. Stewart, ii. 250. Hist. Syst. i. 79. Réflexions Politiques sur les Finances et le Commerce, (par M. du Tot,) ii. 109. Examen du livre intitulé Réflexions Politiques sur les Finances et le Commerce, (par M. du Verney,) i. 299.

Law was named Director-General, and branches were fixed at Lyons, Rochelle, Tours, Orléans, and Amiens.[19]

Thus the bank, being placed in the king's hands, departed from the principles of private and mercantile credit, upon which Mr. Law had originally fixed it, and proceeded upon those of public credit, which, in an absolute monarchy, as France then was, is no other than that of the Sovereign, and consequently cannot be depended upon. To add to the evil, the tenor of the notes was changed, and ran thus: 'The bank promises to pay the bearer, at sight,—livres in silver coin, value received.' By this alteration the money in the notes could not but keep pace with that in the coin, both being equally affected with every arbitrary variation made upon the latter. Mr. Law did all he could to prevent this alteration: it however took place, and the credit of the notes of the Royal Bank became as good as that of the General Bank notes, although the crowns in the latter contained a fixed and positive value, while the livres in the former could, at any time, be reduced, at the pleasure of the Monarch, the debtor in them, to the value of halfpence. Of these notes, there were to the amount of 1000 millions of livres fabricated between the 5th January and 29th December 1719. In February 1720, the Royal Bank was incorporated with the Company of the Indies; and from that incorporation, to the 1st of May following, there were no less than 1,696,400,000 livres more fabricated in notes, making altogether a total of 2,696,400,000 livres in paper money, of which vast sum 2,235,083,590 livres were in circulation on the 29th of May 1720, when the bank stopped payment, as will be hereafter mentioned.[20]

19. Examen, i. 226.

20. Stewart, ii. 240. The notes were of four denominations, *viz* of 10,000, 1000, 100, and 10 livres, none being issued for any other sums. The number of each sort was as follows:

After the establishment of the General Bank, Mr. Law began to lay open the plan of that great and stupendous project he had long meditated, known by the name of The Mississippi System, which, for a while, turned the heads of the French, and attracted the attention of all Europe. The scheme was no less than the vesting of the whole privileges, effects, and possessions of all the foreign trading companies, the great farms, the mint, the general receipt of the king's revenues, and the management and property of the bank, in one great company, who thus having in their hands all the trade, taxes, and royal revenues, might be enabled to multiply the notes of the bank to any extent they pleased, doubling, or even trebling at will the circulating cash of the kingdom, and, by the immensity of their funds, possessed of a power to carry the foreign trade, and the culture of the colonies, to a height altogether impracticable by any other means. The outlines of this plan being laid before the regent, met, it would seem, with the approbation of that prince, as measures were taken for the establishment of the proposed company, and directions issued for making the requisite grants to enable them to commence their operations.

Accordingly, by letters patent dated in August 1717, a commercial company was erected, under the name of the Company of the West, to whom was granted the whole province of Louisiana, a country watered throughout its whole extent

113,400 of	10,000 livres each	1,134,000,000
1,223,200 of	1000 livres each	1,223,200,000
2,992,000 of	100 livres each	299,200,000
4,000,000 of	10 livres each	40,000,000
		2,696,400,000

By edict of 19th September, 1720, notes of 50 livres each, to the extent of 50,000,000 livres, were directed to be made, in order to facilitate the changing of the large notes into small ones.

by the great river Mississippi; from which last circumstance, its subsequent operations came, by way of distinction, to be included under the general name of THE MISSISSIPPI SYSTEM. Of this company 200,000 actions,[21] were issued, rated at 500 livres each, and the subscription for them was ordered to be paid in *billets d'état*. These papers were at that time in such discredit, by reason of the bad payment of their interest, that 500 livres nominal value in them would not have yielded in the market more than 150 or 160 livres; but in the subscription they were taken at their full value; which could not fail to operate as a very tempting bait to the holders to lay them out in the purchase of shares. The company thus became creditors to the king in the sum of 100 millions of livres, the annual rent of which was fixed at the rent of four percent; the first year's interest to be employed for commercial purposes, and the annual rents of the following years to be allotted for paying regularly the dividend, at the rate of twenty livres per annum each share, exclusive of their proportion of the profits of the trade.[22]

Of this Company of the West, Mr. Law, (who had now advanced so high in the regent's favour, that the whole ministerial power was reckoned to be divided among him, the Abbé Dubois, minister for foreign affairs, and M. d'Argenson, keeper of the seals,) was named director general. The actions were eagerly sought after, Louisiana having been represented as a region abounding in gold and silver, of a fertile soil, capable of every sort of cultivation. Such was the rage for speculation that the unimproved parts of that country were sold for 30,000 livres the square league, at which rate, many purchased to the extent of 600,000 livres; vigorous preparations were made for fitting out vessels to transport thither labourers and workmen

21. Shares of the company.

22. Examen, i. 211. Stewart, ii. 235.

of every kind; and the demand for *billets d'état*, in order to purchase shares, occasioned the former to rise to their full nominal value.[23]

The farmers general of the national revenues now taking the alarm, the four brothers Paris, principal managers of that powerful body, acting under the patronage of M. d'Argenson, who had become jealous of Mr. Law's credit with the regent, formed a project to establish an association to advance large sums secured on the farms and the other branches of the public revenue. This project, which was an awkward imitation of Mr. Law's system, and on account of its opposition thereto called the *Anti-Système*, came to nothing; and on the 4th of September 1718, the farm of tobacco was made over to the Company of the West, who agreed to pay 2,020,000 livres additional rent to the king. On the 15th of December following, they acquired the charter and effects of the Senegal Company; but by far the most important grant was that made in May 1719, when an edict was published, transferring to them the exclusive privilege of trading to the East Indies, China, and the South Seas, together with all the possessions and effects belonging to the China and India Companies, on condition of paying the lawful debts of these companies now dissolved. The Company of the West assumed, on this occasion, the title of the Company of the Indies; 50,000 new shares were ordered to be constituted, rated at 550 livres each, payable in coin, to be employed partly in satisfying the creditors of the old companies, and partly in building vessels, and in other preparations for carrying on the trade. The price of actions quickly rose to 1000 livres, the hopes of the public being raised by the favourable prospects of possessing a very lucrative branch of commerce.[24]

On the 25th of July 1719, the mint was made over to the

23. Mémoires du Maréchal Duc de Richelieu, iii. 26

24. Hist. Syst. i. 110. Examen, i. 241. Stewart, ii. 254.

Company of the Indies, for a consideration of 50 millions of livres, to be paid to the king within fifteen months; and 50,000 new shares, rated at 1000 livres each, were directed to be issued, in order to raise that sum. On the 27th of August following, the regent took the great farms out of the hands of the farmers general, and made over the lease to the Company of the Indies, on their agreeing to pay 3,500,000 livres additional rent for them; thus relieving the people from the exactions of that powerful body, under whose management the taxes became quite intolerable, not so much from their own weight, as the oppressive mode of levying them. On the 31st of the same month, the company obtained the general receipt of other branches of the king's revenue. When they had acquired all these grants, and had thus concentrated in themselves the whole foreign trade and possessions of France, and the collection and management of all the royal revenues of that kingdom, they promised an annual dividend of 200 livres on every share; the consequence of which was, that the price of actions instantly rose in the market to 5000 livres, the public ran upon the last creation of 50,000 with such eagerness, that nearly double the requisite sum was subscribed for, and the greatest interest was exerted, and every stratagem put in practice, to secure places in that subscription. The names of the stockholders were not declared for some weeks, and during that interval, according to Lord Stair, Mr. Law's door was kept shut, while the first quality in France appeared on foot in hundreds, before his house in the Place Vendôme.[25]

The company now came under an obligation to lend the king, in order that he might pay off his creditors, the sum of 1500 millions of livres, at the rate of three percent per annum, and to this rate the interest of the 100 millions formerly lent to

25. Examen, ii. 245. Lord Stair's Letters, in the Hardwicke Collection of State Papers, ii. 597.

his Majesty, (in *billets d'état* on the first fabrication of actions, at four percent,) was also reduced; the king consequently had to pay them, in all, 48 millions per year. To raise this sum of 1500 millions, there were, in the months of September and October 1719, 300,000 new actions created, the subscription for which was fixed at 5000 livres each. The actions were thus brought to their full number of 600,000, (for it is unnecessary to take any notice of 24,000 more fabricated on the 4th of October 1719, by the private orders of the regent, but afterwards suppressed,) and to answer the dividends upon these the company had, according to some, the following annual revenue:

	Livres
Interest paid by the King to the company	48,000,000
Profits upon the great farms	15,000,000
Ditto upon the mint	4,000,000
Ditto upon the farm of tobacco	2,000,000
Ditto upon the general receipt of taxes	1,500,000
Ditto upon their trade	10,000,000

This annual revenue came a total of 80,500,000 livres, open to be improved by the extension of their commerce abroad, and by a good administration at home. Other writers on the subject, however, computed the annual revenue of this great company at no less than 131 millions, *viz* 48 millions interest from the king, 39 millions profits upon the farms, the mint, and the receipt of taxes, and 44 millions profits upon their trade; in which case they could well afford a dividend of even more than 200 livres on every share.[26]

The cupidity which these prospects of immense profit in some measure, but principally the prodigious fortunes acquired by the original proprietors, excited among all ranks, was such as no nation had ever before witnessed. A universal infatuation

26. Stewart, ii. 257. Réfl. Politiq. i. 271.

for the acquisition of shares in the India Company now seemed to occupy the whole kingdom, from the lowest of the people up to magistrates, prelates, and princes.[27] This infatuation, of

---

27. The following extract from a commission of the office of Comptroller General of the finances by Mr. John Law, a satirical piece, will illustrate what is stated above of the infatuation of all ranks to engage in the Mississippi:-

Les plaisans viremens,
Et continuels changemens
Que l'on a vu dans le Royaume
De Quincampoix et de Vendôme,
Et Principauté de Soissons,
Ou l'achat et le dividend
Causoient un rumeur si grande,
Qu'on ne vit jamais tant de rats
Obséder gens de tous états;
Mari, femme, garçon, et fille,
Laquais, servantes, la famille
En un mot, sans rien excepter,
Venit jouer et blanqueter.
Là de tous pais et provinces,
Marchands, magistrats, artisans,
Prélats, guerriers, et courtisans,
Ducs et pairs, même des princes,
Non du pais, mais bien forains,
Accouroient comme des essaims,
Malgré vent, grêle, pluye, et crotte,
Pour y jouer à la marotte,
En beaux et bons deniers comptans,
Centre les voleurs calotines,
Dont la France et terres voisines
Se pourront souvenir long terns.

Mémoires de Pollnitz, ii. 241.

which, at the present day, we can scarcely form a conception, increased in proportion to the difficulty of succeeding in that view; for the whole 300,000 actions of the last fabrication, being, by a particular agreement, kept up in order to be sold to the regent, who had also got possession of 100,000 of these formerly issued, no more than 200,000 remained in the hands of the public, and only a part thereof, quite inadequate to the demand, was now brought to market. The frenzy prevailed so far, that the whole nation, clergy and laity, peers and plebeians, statesmen, princes, nay, even ladies, who had or could procure money for that purpose, turned stockjobbers, outbidding each other with such avidity, that in November 1719, the price of shares rose, after some fluctuations, to above 10,000 livres each; more than sixty times the sum they originally sold for, when the discredit of the *billets d'état* is taken into the account.[28]

So much indeed were the people interested in this business, that nothing was talked of but actions, and every place echoed with Mississippi and the Rue Quincampoix.[29] All classes appeared to have but one object, the acquisition of shares of the India Company; mechanics laid by their work, tradesmen forsook their shops, all degrees entirely neglected their profession and employments, to embark in this new occupation; and the few that did not proceed to that extreme, conducted themselves in a manner calculated to manifest the little concern they took in affairs foreign to the Mississippi. One of this last description, M. Chirac, principal physician to the regent, on his way to visit a female patient, having been informed that the price of actions was falling, was so affected by that piece of news that he could think of nothing else; and, accordingly, while holding the lady's pulse, kept exclaiming, 'O good God, it falls, it falls.' The invalid, naturally alarmed,

28. Siècle de Louis XV par Voltaire, iii. 11.

29. The street where the stock jobbing was at first carried on.

began to ring the bell with all her force, crying out that she was a dead woman, and had almost expired with apprehension, till the doctor assured her that her pulse was in a very good state, but that his mind ran so much upon actions, that he came to utter the expressions that terrified her, in reference to the fall of their value. That learning herself could not shield her votaries from the infection, appears from the following circumstance. M. de la Mothe and the Abbé Terrasson, two of the ablest scholars in France, conversing together on the madness of the Mississippi adventurers, congratulated themselves on their superiority over all weaknesses of that nature; and indulged themselves in ridiculing the folly of the votaries of the fickle goddess. But it so happened that they met, not long afterwards, face to face in the Rue Quincampoix; at first they endeavoured to avoid each other, but finding that impracticable, put the best look possible on the matter, rallied each other, and separated in order to make the most advantageous bargains they could. The courtiers, according to their usual custom of following implicitly the royal example, engaged so deeply in this business, that it was said only five persons of that description, (the Maréchal de Villeroi and de Villars, the Ducs de St. Simon and de la Rochefoucault, and the Chancellor,) had kept free from the contagion. The Maréchal Duc de Richelieu relates, that those who did not embark in the Mississippi were looked upon as no better than cowards or fools.[30]

The negotiations for the sale and purchase of actions were, at first, carried on in the Rue Quincampoix, to the no small emolument of the occupiers of houses in that street, lodgings letting at so high a rate, that a house rented at 800 livres per year, yielded from 6000 to 16,000 livres per month, and even single apartments were let at the rate of one pistole per day.

30. Fragm. ii. 273. Duclos, Mémoires Secrètes sur les Regnes de Louis XIV et de Louis XV, ii. 114. Richelieu, iii. 25. Pollnitz, ii. 240.

A cobbler, who wrought in a stall formed of planks set up against the garden wall of M. Tourton the banker, bethought himself of furnishing his little shop with a few chairs for the accommodation of the ladies that came out of curiosity to see the crowd; by which, and by supplying the brokers with pens and paper, he earned no less than 200 livres per day. At length, it becoming impossible for all to procure even that humble accommodation, most of the stockjobbers transacted their business in the open air. So great was the concourse, that all the avenues leading into the Rue Quincampoix were quite choked up by break of day, and the crowd still continued to increase till the evening bell was rung, when they were obliged to be driven away by force.[31] It was, therefore, proposed to remove the business to a more commodious situation, and the execution of this measure was accelerated by the murder and robbery of a rich stockjobber, committed on the 22nd of March 1720, by a young Flemish nobleman, Count Horn, and two associates, who, under pretence of bargaining for actions, conducted the unfortunate man to a tavern in the Rue de Venise, and there dispatched him with a poignard. The Count, who was only 22 years of age, being taken the same day, was condemned to be broken alive on the wheel; and this sentence was accordingly inflicted in the Place de Grève on the 26th of March, notwithstanding he was allied to several sovereign houses, and related to the Duc d'Orléans himself. The greatest interest was made to save his life; but all solicitations on that head were unavailing, Mr. Law convincing the regent of the

31. The Memoirs of the Regency (vol. ii 331.) notice a hump-backed man, who in the course of a few days acquired 150,000 livres by letting out his hump as a writing desk to the brokers in the Rue Quincampoix. A plan of Paris being about this time laid before Louis XV then only ten years of age, the young Monarch found fault with it, because that street was not distinguished from the others by gilding.

absolute necessity of making a severe example of that criminal, at a time when many carried their whole fortunes in their pockets.[32]

The very day that this murder was committed, the council issued an edict, expressly prohibiting all persons, of what degree soever, from assembling in the Rue Quincampoix, for the purpose of selling or buying stock, and forbidding the keeping of offices for their reception in that street. For some time afterwards, the stockjobbers and brokers were left to meet where they could; but in the month of June, the paper traffic was transferred to the Place Vendôme. The superb hotels of which that magnificent square (or rather octagon) consisted, not being calculated for the establishment of offices for transacting business, a number of tents were, for that purpose, pitched in the area. Of these, some served for the accommodation of the stockjobbers, others were destined for places of refreshment, and a third set was occupied by gamesters playing at quadrille, and drawing lotteries of jewels. All the world flocked to this spot, ladies of the highest quality delighted to walk there in the evening, and the concourse was so great, that the famous Fair of Beaucaire appeared a desert in comparison. The excessive noise so prodigious a resort could not fail to occasion, was productive of so much disturbance, that the Chancellor complained he was thereby prevented from attending to the causes in the Chancery in the Place Vendôme. Mr. Law thereupon agreed with the Prince of Carignan for the purchase of the Hotel de Soissons, at the enormous price, as is said, of 1,400,000 livres, and in the gardens belonging to that edifice, above 600 pavilions, each rated at 500 livres per month, were disposed in regular order, beautifully interspersed with trees and fountains. To oblige the brokers to make use of them, an ordinance was issued,

32. Mémoires de la Régence, ii. 331, 392. Duclos, ii. 96. Hist. Syst. iii. 119-134, 182, 194.

prohibiting, under severe penalties, any bargain for stock to be concluded, except in one of these pavilions, and the business was accordingly carried on there till the 8th of November 1720, when all persons were finally forbidden to assemble for the purpose of stock jobbing in any place whatever.[33]

The unexampled rise of the price of actions afforded an opportunity to several obscure and low individuals to acquire at once princely fortunes; and these rapid revolutions could not fail to be productive of many laughable occurrences, such as the following:—A footman had gained so much that he provided himself with a fine carriage; but the first day it came to the door, he, instead of stepping into the vehicle, mounted up to his old station behind. Another, in a similar predicament, brought himself well off by pretending he got up only to see if there was room on the back for two or three more lacqueys, whom he was resolved to hire instantly. Mr. Law's coachman had made so great a fortune, that he asked a to be dismissed from his service, which was readily granted, on condition of procuring another as good as himself. The man thereupon brought two coachmen, told his master they were both excellent drivers, and desired him to make choice of one, at the same time saying that he would take the other for his own carriage. One night at the opera, a Mademoiselle de Begond observing a lady enter, magnificently dressed, and covered with diamonds, jogged her mother, and said, I am much mistaken if this fine lady is not Mary our cook. The report spread through the theatre till it came to the ears of the lady, who, coming up to Madame de Begond, said, 'I am indeed Mary your cook, I have gained large sums in the Rue Quincampoix, I love fine clothes and fine jewels, and am accordingly dressed in them. I have paid for every thing, am in debt to nobody, and pray what has any person in this place to say to this?' At another time, some persons of

33. Hist. Syst. iii. 168, iv. 5, 72. vi. 69. Duclos, ii. 115.

quality beholding a gorgeous figure alight from a most splendid equipage, and inquiring what great lady that was, one of her lacqueys answered, 'A woman who has tumbled from a garret into a carriage.' One of these upstarts, finding himself enriched beyond his utmost expectations, hastened to a coachmaker's, and ordered a berlin to be made in the finest taste, lined with the richest crimson velvet and gold fringe, and went away after leaving 4000 livres as earnest. The coach maker running after him to inquire what arms were to be put on the carriage, was answered, 'Oh, the finest, the finest by all means.' A quondam footman, sitting in a newly acquired carriage, having his way impeded by another belonging to an officer, their servants quarrelled, and the former having made use of some improper expressions, the officer obliged him to alight; and putting his hand to his sword, the other took to his heels, crying out, Brethren of the livery, come to my assistance. But, perhaps, the drollest circumstance that occurred, was what happened to one Brignaud, (son of a baker at Thoulouse,) who being desirous of having a superb service of plate, purchased the whole articles exposed for sale in the shop of a goldsmith for 400,000 livres, and sent them home to his wife, with orders to set them out properly for supper, to which he had invited many persons of distinction. The lady, not understanding the business, arranged the plate according to her fancy, and without regard to their real use; so that when supper was announced, the guests could not forbear from indulging in peals of laughter to see the soup served up in a bason for receiving the offerings at church, the sugar in a censer, and chalices holding the place of salt-sellers, while most of the other articles were more suited to a toilet than a sideboard.[34]

---

34. Mem, Reg. ii. 328-330. Hist. Syst. iii. 72. It may perhaps require some explanation how so many low persons should acquire large fortunes from nothing, in so short a time; but independent of the rise in the

Mr. Law now blazed a meteor of unequalled splendour, having arrived at a pitch of power and consequence, (*summa ad fastigia rerum*,) that required a strength of intellect almost supernatural to be able to support undazzled. He saw himself perpetually followed by, and his levee constantly crowded with, Princes, Dukes, and Peers, Marshals and Prelates, who all humbled themselves before his shrine with the utmost submission, while he treated them at times in a style of consummate haughtiness. Of this, Archibald, Duke of Argyle used to relate a remarkable

---

price of actions, various indeed were the ways of doing so during the Mississippi contagion. Some, either unable or unwilling to go to the Rue Quincampoix to dispose of their shares, trusted them to others, who received orders to sell for a certain sum. On their arrival, they commonly found the price risen, and without scruple put the difference into their own pockets. A gentleman falling sick sent his servant to dispose of 250 shares, for 8000 livres each; and he sold them at the rate of 10,000 livres, making a profit of 500,000 livres, which he appropriated to himself, and by other lucky adventures increased that sum to upwards of 2 millions. A person deputed to sell 200 shares for another, kept himself concealed for some days, during which time their price rose so high that he cleared near a million of livres of profit, giving back to his employer, who had been hunting him in vain, only the market rate of the day on which he was sent to dispose of the actions. One De Josier, trusted with the like number of shares, to sell for 550 livres each, disappeared, but coming back when the system was at its height, profited immensely by disposing of them at a price greatly advanced. It is likewise to be observed, that several fluctuations in the price of actions happened even in the same day, insomuch that it was not unusual for a stockjobber, by selling with one hand and buying with the other, to come out of the Rue Quincampoix in the evening, with the same number of shares he had carried with him in the morning, and 200,000 livres of profit. Gambling also was carried to such a height, that it was common for one to lose or win above a million in a day. Hist. Syst. ii. 166.

instance. His Grace, then Earl of Ilay, going to wait upon Mr. Law by appointment, found the antechambers filled with many of the highest quality in France; but being, by special orders, admitted into his private apartments, beheld the great man writing what, from the number and rank of those left to wait his leisure, he naturally concluded to be dispatches of the utmost consequence. Upon mentioning these surmises to his old friend, it was with no small surprise his Lordship learned that he was only writing to his gardener at Lauriston to plant cabbages on a particular spot. After this important epistle was concluded, he desired the Earl to play a party at piquet, and they accordingly sat down to that game, at which they continued for a good while, till at length the great man thought proper to give orders for the admission of his humble supplicants.[35]

The Baron de Pollnitz observes, in his memoirs, that he has seen Dukes and Peers of France waiting in Mr. Law's antechambers like the meanest subjects, and that at last there

35. Notwithstanding this well-authenticated anecdote, it appears from the Mémoires de Pollnitz, and Madame's Letters, that Mr. Law was by no means puffed up with the adulation lavishly bestowed on him; but that in general he behaved in an extremely polite and civil manner to every body. He was particularly attentive to such of his countrymen as were properly recommended to him. Dr. Alexander Monro of Auchinbowie, Professor of Anatomy in the University of Edinburgh, visiting Paris at this period, waited upon Mr. Law, to whom he had letters of introduction. His reception from that minister was highly flattering; and he was accustomed to say, that the Comptroller General was one of the easiest, most affable, and best behaved men he had ever seen, and bestowed so much time and attention on him as was perfectly astonishing, when the number, the variety, and the importance of the pursuits in which he was then engaged, were considered. (Communicated by the late Mrs. Philp, wife of James Philp of Greenlaw, Judge of Admiralty in Scotland, daughter of Dr. Monro.)

was no getting near him without feeing the Swiss porters for entrance at the gate, the lacqueys for admittance into the antechamber, and the valets for the privilege of access to his presence chamber or closet. The audiences too were very short, and the people were quickly dismissed with very little merchandise for a great deal of money.[36]

Those were now reckoned supremely blessed, who could obtain one word or one smile from that sole dispenser of the favours of fortune; and nothing could afford a disinterested spectator more amusement than to observe the people running in crowds, pressing each other to death, only to be seen by Mr. Law or his son, as if one of their glances had the power to enrich those upon whom it happened to fall. The former was so much plagued with suitors for actions, that he could hardly get a moment of rest either by day or night, every kind of stratagem being put in practice, and no money spared, to procure admission into his presence, even at the most unseasonable hours. Of all his solicitors, the most importunate were the ladies, who pestered him incessantly. Madame, the regent's mother, in one of her letters, asserts that 'Si Laws vouloit, les femmes Françoises lui baiseroient la derrière,' all ideas of decency and delicacy being completely absorbed by the more potent power of avarice; and she gives the following very striking instance of the truth of her assertion: 'Un jour qu'il donnoit audience à des dames, il voulut se retirer, ayant un si grand besoin de pisser qu'il n'y tenoit plus. Ces dames lui retinrent, il leur enfin fit confidence du besoin qui le pressoit. Oh, si ce n'est que cela, dirent elles, cela ne fait rien; pissez toujours, et écoutez nous. Et elles resterent avec lui pendant tout le tems !'[37] According to the Maréchal Duc de Richelieu, 'Law jouissoit alors à Paris du respect de tous les ordres de l'état, les Duchesses lui baisoient

36. Duclos, ii. 72. Pollnitz, ii. 244.

37. Fragm. ii. 274.

les mains, et les Princes lui rendoient fréquemment des visites. Pressé un jour d'audience par un grand concours de personnes qui avoient à lui parler, et voulant se retirer pour des besoins urgens, les dames lui dirent, Monseigneur, si vous n'avez d'autre besoin que celui de pisser, ne vous en allez pas, pissez ici, et écoutez nous. Law sans s'étonner usa, de la permission, et pissa en pleine assemblée.'[38]

Madame relates other instances of the importunity of her sex. One Madame de Bouchu had strained every nerve to be admitted to a dinner at Madame de Simiani's, where Mr. Law was to be present; but all her endeavours were ineffectual, it being known he did not choose to see her. She then bethought herself of ordering her coach to be driven before the house at dinner time, and directed the coachmen and lacqueys to give the alarm of fire, which made all the guests rise from table and run into the street. On Mr. Law's appearance, she jumped out of her carriage to accost him, but he took to his heels the moment he beheld her face.[39]

Another lady, more adventurous, gave orders to her coachman to overturn her carriage whenever he came near Mr. Law. She, however, was the first that perceived him, whereupon she roared out, 'Overturn the carriage now, you rascal, overturn the carriage.' The man did so accordingly; and Mr. Law courteously coming to her assistance, the lady confessed that she had given such orders, in hopes thereby to have a chance of procuring the honour of speaking to him, an honour to which she could not otherwise have presumed to aspire.[40]

An old lady was so particularly eager and importunate in discourse with Mr. Law, that not attending sufficiently to her expressions, in place of saying, 'Faites moi un concession,' she

38. Richelieu, iii. 374.

39. Fragm. ii. 275.

40. *Ibid.* ii. 276.

addressed him in these words, 'Ah Monsieur, faites moi, je vous en prie, une conception.' He could not refrain from laughing at this droll slip of the tongue, and replied, 'Vous venez trop tard, il n'y a pas moyen à présent.'[41]

Mr. Law's family and connections participated of this universal adulation and courtship. The regent wanting a Duchess to perform a particular piece of etiquette, that of conducting his daughter, the Princess of Modena, to Genoa, somebody told him, if he wished to make a selection, to send to Lady Catherine Law's, and he would be sure of finding all the Duchesses in the kingdom there; although the insolence of that lady was so great, that she was accustomed to say there was not a more tiresome animal in the world than a Duchess. Her son had the high honour of being named to dance with the young King, Louis XV in a most superb ballet, directed by the Maréchal de Villeroi.

Miss Law, though then extremely young, was asked in marriage by several of the first families in Europe, particularly by the prince of Tarente; and having issued cards of invitation for a ball, every person who pretended to any distinction thought it incumbent upon them to attend it. The Nuncio, coming among the first, paid his compliments to the young queen of the assembly by kissing her; which was, even at that time, reckoned an extraordinary mark of condescension in the representative of the Pontiff.[42]

The rage for speculating in the French funds was not confined to that kingdom, several persons of the first consequence in Britain engaging therein. The following letter, from the Earl of Ilay to Mrs. Howard, afterwards Countess of Suffolk, dated Paris, September, 1719, affords striking examples of the stock jobbing infatuation which at this period had seized all ranks

41. Fragm, ii. 278.

42. Duclos, ii. 73. Hist. Syst. ii. 19. Fragm. ii. 271.

and both sexes in England and France: 'Notwithstanding the politeness of this place, I have no other way to answer the beginning of your letter but by a flat contradiction; 'troublesome,—impertinent,—new favours,' as to me, is impossible, and even as to others, I have too good an opinion of mankind, that those who have least merit, I believe, would think themselves happy in receiving your commands. To show you, in two words, how the thanks you mention are owing on my side, consider that you might have had the friendship of many considerable men by being my enemy, and I could only have received the precarious nauseous professions of one silly woman by not being your friend. I have laid out the money you bid me. It is very difficult in a letter to give you an idea of the funds of this country; but in fact every body has made estates that have been concerned in them for four or five months. As a little instance of this, cousin Jack[43] has got, I believe, near £10,000, and has lost the half of that sum by a timorous silly bargain he made; for my part, I came after all was in a manner over, and as I never meddle with these matters, I do nothing but buy books and gimcracks.[44] It is true it is now very late, and yet, by what I am informed by him who knows all, and does all, I am of opinion that whatever sum you remit here may be turned to great profit. The stocks are now at 950, and if no accidents happen of mortality, it is probable they will be 1500 in a short time. The money I laid out for you was 5000 livres, as a subscriber to the fifty millions of stock lately added, of which the tenth part only is paid down, so that 5000 is the first payment of 50,000 livres. The subscription was full, but Mr. Law was so kind as allow it me; some of the subscribers have

43. Probably Colonel John Campbell of Mamore, afterwards fourth Duke of Argyle, the husband of Mary Bellenden.

44. We shall see presently that this assertion is contradicted in this very letter. Lord Ilay was deep in the Mississippi Scheme.

already sold their subscriptions for 230, that is their own money back again, and one hundred thirty percent profit. Whatever you think fit to do, you may bid Middleton remit to me so many livres, I shall acknowledge the receipt of them and do the best I can. You will think that the levity of this country has turned my head when I tell you your Master[45] might, within these few months, have made himself richer than his father. As late as I came, I can tell you, in secret, that I am pretty well.'[46]

The situation of France, in November 1719, is thus described by a contemporary writer: 'The bank notes were just so much real value which credit and confidence had created in favour of the state. Upon their appearance, plenty immediately displayed herself through all the towns and all the country; she relieved our citizens and labourers from the oppression of debts which indigence had obliged them to contract; she enabled the king to liberate himself from great part of his debts, and to make over to his subjects more than fifty-two millions of livres of taxes which had been imposed in the years preceding 1719; and more than thirty-five millions of other duties extinguished during the Regency. This plenty sunk the rate of interest, crushed the usurer, carried the value of lands to 80 and 100 years purchase, raised up stately edifices both in town and country, repaired the old houses which were falling to ruin, improved the soil, gave an additional relish to every fruit produced by the earth. Plenty recalled those citizens whom misery had forced to seek their livelihood abroad. In a word, riches flowed in from every quarter; gold, silver, precious stones, ornaments of every kind which contribute to luxury and magnificence, came to us from every country in Europe. Whether these prodigies or marvellous

45. The Prince of Wales, afterwards King George II. A subsequent letter from the Earl of Ilay, dated 16th January, 1720, leads one to believe that this hint was not thrown away.

46. Suffolk Letters, p.42-45.

effects were produced by art, by confidence, by fear, or by whim if you please, one must agree, that that art, that confidence, that fear, or that whim, had operated all these realities, which the ancient administration never could have produced. Thus far the System had produced nothing but good; every thing was commendable and worthy of admiration.'[47]

Such, according to an eyewitness, were the advantages resulting to the French, from the establishment of public credit among them. Money now circulated in the utmost profusion, all ranks of people indulged themselves in every species of luxury, and the prices of commodities rose excessively.[48] Strangers of every nation flocked in great numbers to Paris to speculate in the stocks, insomuch that it was computed there were no less than 305,000 foreigners in that capital in November 1719, the consequence of which was a prodigious influx of wealth into the kingdom. The very granaries and magazines were filled with inhabitants; and so great was the crowd of equipages set up, that it was scarcely possible to pass through any street without the utmost difficulty, and even danger of hurting or killing some of the numerous passengers. Fine clothes were so much sought after, that the shops in Paris were completely stripped of all the velvet and cloth of gold exposed for sale. On this account,

47. Réfl. Politiq. ii. 330.

48. The ell or cloth of fifteen livres sold for fifty livres, and a pound of coffee rose from fifty sols to eighteen livres. Artificers who used to work for fifteen sols, now would not take less than three livres per day. By an account taken from the books of the silversmiths of Paris, it appeared, that in the course of three months they had made no less than 120,000 dozens of plates, besides dishes answerable; reckoning each dozen at 60, the total value of them alone comes to £7,200,000. Such was the prodigality of some of the stockjobbers, that an instance occurred where one of them gave 200 livres for a single wood-hen for his dinner; and green peas at 100 pistoles the pint have been served up at some tables.

several remarked, that the winter season of this year exhibited more splendour and brilliancy than the finest summer ever seen before.[49]

When this apparently flourishing posture of affairs was contrasted with the lamentable situation in which France was plunged at the death of Louis XIV, it is no wonder that Mr. Law, who was considered as the author of all that prosperity, should be reckoned, as it were, the saviour of the kingdom. He was perfectly idolized by the people, who looked on him as no way inferior to the king and the regent, the mob being accustomed to cry out, whenever he appeared in public, Long live Mr. Law. The popular veneration was still further increased by his making, along with his son and daughter, a public profession of the Roman Catholic religion, which was done with great pomp in the church of the Récollets at Melun, in December 1719.[50] In order to manifest his zeal and sincerity, he communicated, and made the bread offering, at St. Roch, his parish church, on Christmas day; and was constituted Honorary Church Warden thereof, in room of the Duc de Noailles, on which occasion he made a present of 500,000 livres to complete the building of that edifice. At this season his liberality to the distressed was boundless; he distributed another sum of 500,000 livres among the English at St. Germain en Laye, whose pensions had been suppressed; and having, some time afterwards, ordered several vessels to be freighted with the finest fish that could be procured, for supplying the inhabitants of Paris during lent, it so happened, that owing to a long continuance of contrary winds, the first ship did not arrive till Easter Eve. He thereupon distributed gratuitously the whole cargo of the fleet among the

49. Hist. Syst. ii. 105, Richelieu, iii. 37.

50. Lady Catherine Law refused to abjure the religion in which she was brought up, and was much distressed at this conduct of her husband and children. Fragm. ii. 281.

mendicant friars and other poor communities. He likewise bestowed vast sums in alms, and contributed largely to hospitals and other charitable foundations, besides making many very valuable presents to individuals.[51]

The only obstacle to his advancement being removed by his conversion, Mr. Law was, on the 5th of January 1720, declared Comptroller General of the Finances of France. Thus the admiring world beheld an obscure foreigner, by the mere force of extraordinary genius and abilities, rise in the course of a few months from a private condition to the high station of Prime Minister of the politest nation in Europe, which he governed for some time with almost absolute power. It must be mentioned, to his honour, that he voluntarily gave up the whole perquisites as well as the salary annexed to his office; and he was so little addicted to luxury and extravagance, as to take care that the most regular order and strictest propriety should be observed in the management of his household, while, at the same time, his dress was remarked for its plainness and simplicity. All ranks now vied with each other in paying court to the new Premier; the Academy of Sciences elected him one of their honorary members, 2nd December 1719;[52] and the followers of the muses spared no pains in culling the choicest flowers of the gardens of Parnassus to form wreaths for adorning his temples, some specimens of which are subjoined.

51. Mem. Reg. ii. 369.

52. After the downfall of the System, the king having declared Mr. Law's election into the Royal Academy void, because his letters of naturalization had not at that time been registered, the Academy, on the 13th August 1721, elected Cardinal Fleury honorary member in his room.

ILLUSTRISSIMO NOBILISSIMOQUE D. D. LAW,
INCOMPARABILIS INGENII VIRO,

EPIGRAMMA.

Pallas inexhaustae praecellens lumine mentis
Concilio in superum talia dicta dedit;
Insuetum tentemus opus, junctique creemus
Mortalem, ingenii qui sit imago mei.
Sese operi accingunt superi, tandemque crearunt
Mortalem optatum, Lawius ille fuit.

DE QUODAM LUDI GENERE APUD
MICISSIPIPPOS.

Luserunt luduntque etiam civesque, ducesque,
Et plebs, externis turbaque missa plagis;
Nemo perdiderat; ditat se quisque; Deorum
Talem quis ludum finxit, Apollo refer.
Consultus, mora nulla fuit, respondit Apollo,
Mortalis finxit, non Deus illud opus.
At cunctos inter mortales fingere ludum
Talem quis poterat?—Lawius unus erat.

EIDEM ILLUSTRISSIMO NOBILISSIMO VIRO,
PHILOSOPHORUM PRINCIPI.

Inventa fecere Sophi sibi nomen ab arte;
Hactenus at solum re sine nomen erat.
Nummos mille modis augendi Lawius artem
Invenit, haec veros ars facit una Sophos.

Obtulit P. St. John, Poeta Regius.

INSCRIPTION ON AN ENGRAVED PORTRAIT OF MR. LAW.

Principe sub recto Gallorum sceptra tenente,
Publica nunc recte Quaestor hie aera regit:
Aeraque tractandi summa perfectus in arte
Et Regem et populum divitem utrumque facit.

At this period, a report was spread that Mr. Law was to be raised to the peerage, by the title of Duc de Tancarville, and that the office of Grand Treasurer was to be revived, and conferred upon him; his native city of Edinburgh, proud of having produced so great a man, transmitted to him the freedom thereof in a gold box of the value of £300 sterling;[53] and he negotiated with Lord Londonderry for the purchase of Pitt's famous diamond, long the brightest jewel in the French crown.[54] The editor of the Letters from Henrietta, Countess of Suffolk, says, that the Earl of Ilay published in December 1719, a treatise formerly written by Mr. Law, with an encomiastic preface from the pen of his Lordship, and this motto from Cicero, '*O terrain illam beatam qui hunc virum exceperit; hanc ingratam si ejecerit, miseram si amiserit.*' A wonderful example of adulation and infatuation! There was printed at the Hague, in 1720: 'Considérations sur le Commerce et sur Pargent, par M. Law, Contrôleur Général des Finances, traduites de l'Anglois,' embellished with a portrait thus inscribed, 'M. Jean Law, Counseiller du Roi en tous ses Conseils, Contrôleur Général des Finances, 1720.

53. In the diploma, which is dated at Edinburgh, 5th August, 1719, he is styled the Right Hon. John Law, Lord and Earl of Tancarville, Director General of the Royal Bank and India Company of the kingdom of France.

54. Mem. Reg. ii. 358. Fragm. ii. 292. Richelieu, iii. 27. Duclos, ii. 134.

Sous l'auguste et sage régence
D'un Prince aimant la bonne foy,
Law consommé dans l'art de régir les finances,
Trouve l'art d'enrichir les sujets et le Roi.

A British nobleman who then visited Paris, said, in a public advertisement, that Mr. Law appeared a Minister far above all the past age had known, the present could conceive, or the future could believe; that he had established public credit in a country that was become a proverb for the breach of it; and that he had shown the French people that Louis XIV was not able, with his unlimited authority, to take more away from, than he had restored to, them.[55]

From the following letter of the Earl of Ilay to Mrs. Howard, dated Paris, 16th January, 1720, it would appear that the Prince of Wales, afterwards King George II had some concern in the Mississippi transactions, and did not disdain to pay court to Mr. Law:

'Since my Lord Belhaven[56] has been here, I have so much taken it for granted that he will have informed his acquaintances of your family of the Paris news, that I thought it idle to repeat it; however, for scribbling sake, I trouble you with this.

It would be very difficult for me to give you any tolerable account of the Mississippi, since I was the last time in France, without writing a pamphlet. Every post I receive from England new terrors concerning it, and, what is really very diverting,

55. Salmon's Chronology, ii. 101.

56. John, third Lord Belhaven, one of the gentlemen of the bed chamber to George, Prince of Wales, appointed governor of Barbados in April 1721, but perished by shipwreck on the Stag Rocks, near the Lizard Point, 17th November, same year. There seems reason to believe, from some of Lord Ilay's expressions, that Lord Belhaven's visit to Paris related to some concern of his royal master with Mr. Law and the French funds.

some are extremely apprehensive of my losing the money I have got, who, to my certain knowledge, are very much mortified at my getting it. I am not insensible of distant dangers which may attend the funds here, and I wish our own were absolutely free from them; but for the objections which have come from even considerable people in England, they prove more that they have learned their own business by rote, than that they have any true notions of the principles of these matters. I know a pretty extraordinary instance of something of this kind, if I could venture to tell; but thus far I may venture to say, that either Mr. Law knows nothing, or some who carry their heads very high in England know less than people imagine.

I wish I had known of a certain compliment paid to Mr. Law by order,[57] before he told it me himself; for I may say to you, in confidence, without vanity, and without impertinence, that it would have been nothing the worse. It has obliged me to enter into a long, disagreeable, and unhappy detail, in order to explain the mystery of endeavouring to make a friend of mine well with him, and yet concealing his errand from him; as soon as I had justified myself, I proceeded to do my duty to my superiors, and that perhaps more than would have been prudent, (in, at least, a volunteer,) if I had not entire confidence in the person I spoke to, and were not master of too much philosophy, and too much money, not to be afraid of doing what I think right. I have often heard of my being *opiniatre*, but I had always this comfort, that if I had any honesty, a little of the other was often very necessary in this world.

Your money matters go on very well, though the actions

---

57. It would seem that Lord Ilay wanted to introduce Lord Belhaven to Mr. Law, as a private friend, while Mr. Law was apprised from some other quarter, by order, that Lord Belhaven was employed by the Prince. The whole affair is sufficiently mysterious, but there can be little doubt that it relates to some transactions between the Prince and Mr. Law.

are fallen from 1900 to 1750; yet the meaning of it is nothing else but people selling their actions in order to buy the new primes, (as they are called,) which are a sort of subscription at 2200, 1000 livres down, and 10,000 six months hence. The government here will find it so much their interest to prevent any persons losing by accepting their offer, that I am of opinion there will be something to be got this way. I do from time to time inform my Lord Belhaven of any thing that occurs to me for his service; and I believe he will say that I have been useful to him. I shall leave this place in a few days. I am, Madam, your slave.'[58]

During these important transactions, and for some years preceding, the place of Ambassador from England to the Court of Paris was filled by the Earl of Stair, a nobleman as much distinguished for courage and conduct in the field, as for ability in the cabinet. Several of his letters to Mr. Craggs, one of the Secretaries of State, are published in the Hardwicke Collection of State Papers; and the following extracts from them will show in what a formidable light his Lordship viewed the power and abilities of his countryman, with whom, it appears, he was on very indifferent terms:

'Supposing I had talents, and that I were fitter to serve you at this court than another, you will be obliged to change your minister. You may depend on it, this court, with their fortune, will change their measures; and they will desire to have a man here that they may be either able to gain or impose upon. You must henceforth look upon Law as the first minister, whose daily discourse is, that he will raise France to a greater height than ever she was, upon the ruin of England and Holland. You may easily imagine I shall not be a minister for his purpose. He is very much displeased with me already, because I did not flatter his vanity by putting into Mississippi. I did not think it

58. Suffolk Letters, p. 45-48

became the king's ambassador to give countenance to such a thing, or an example to others to withdraw their effects from England to put them into the stocks here, which would have been readily followed by many. I have been in the wrong to myself to the value of thirty or forty thousand pounds, which I might very easily have gained if I had put myself, as others did, into Mr. Law's hands; but I thought it my duty, considering my station, not to do so.

'He' (the Abbé Dubois) told me, that if some people prevailed, measures would be changed; that Torcy took the ascendant very much, and that the regent discovered a great partiality towards him; and that, if it continued a little longer, he, the Abbe, would lay down. I am sure Law is in this thing, for he will be for removing every thing that does not absolutely depend upon him, and that can in any manner stand in his way to be first minister. Law's heart has been set upon that from the beginning; and we stand too directly in the way of his ambitious views for France, to imagine that a good understanding can subsist long between the nations, if he comes to govern absolutely.[59]

They tell the regent that he has now overcome all his difficulties; that France is now greater, and in a more flourishing condition than ever she was; and that to make his court to the nation, he has nothing to do now but to enter into the ancient maxims and political views of the crown, and to make all Europe depend on France, or to crush those that stand in the way.

I come now to take notice of another thing to you, which, in my opinion, is very much to be minded, and that is the spirit, behaviour, and discourse of the man whom, from henceforth, you must look upon as the first minister, and that is Mr. Law. He in all his discourse pretends he will set France much higher than ever she was before, and put her in a condition to give

59. 1st September 1719.

the law to all Europe; that he can ruin the trade and credit of England and Holland whenever he pleases; that he can break our bank whenever he has a mind; and our East India Company.[60] He said publicly the other day at his own table, when Lord Londonderry was present, that there was but one great kingdom in Europe, and one great town, and that was France and Paris. He told Pitt that he would bring down our East India stock, and entered into articles with him to sell him, at twelve months hence, £100,000 of stock at eleven percent under the current price. You may imagine what we have to apprehend from a man of this temper, who makes no scruple to declare such views, and who will have all the power and all the credit at this court.'[61]

'Il y a quelques jours qu'on m'avertit, de très bonne part, que M. Law avoit dit à M. le Duc d'Orléans que c'étoit moi qui avois eté cause de l'attaque qu'on avoit faite en dernier lieu sur la banque. Sur cet avis je pris la résolution de m'éclaircir sur ce fait avec M. le Duc d'Orléans, et je tournois la conversation de manière que S. A. R. me dit qu'on l'avoit dit que j'étois cause de l'attaque sur la banque. Je lui dis, Monseigneur, je sçais que M. Law vous a tenu tel discours, et je suis bien aise d'avoir l'occasion de prouver a V. A. R. qu'il est absolument faux dans toutes ses circonstances. Il est très vrai que les sujets du Roi mon maître ont un très grand poids d'argent dans ce pays ici, qu'il m'auroit eté fort aisé de faire porter contre la banque. Mais, s'il est vrai, qui ni moi, ni aucun sujet du Roi ait porté des billets pourétre changéz à la banque; si nous n'avons pas porté les actions sur la place, pour les faire baisser; s'il est vrai que je n'ai eu nulle communication avec ceux qui ont couru sur la banque, V. A. R. doit étre convaincue que le discours de M. Law est

60. The reader will observe the similarity between these expressions, and the boastings of Bonaparte in the plenitude of his power.

61. 9th September 1719.

non seulement faux, mais que c'est la calomnie du monde la plus atroce, et la plus indigne; laquelle ne tend pas seulement à tromper V. A. R. sur mon chapitre, qui suis son serviteur affidé de tout temps, par reconnoissance et par affection; mais qui tend à brouiller V. A. R. avec le Roi mon maître, qui est votre meilleur ami, et votre meilleur allié; car je Sais que M. Law a dit, au même temps, que ce que je faisois à cet égard, je la faisois par ordre de ma cour.

Or, Monseigneur, si M. Law ne peut prouver à V. A. R. qu'il y a un de ces trois faits vrai, comme j'avance hardiment à V. A. R. qu'ils sont faux touts trois, il doit passer dans l'esprit de V. A. R. pour un calomniateur, qui a dessein de la tromper dans des choses de la dernière conséquence. Mais, ce n'est pas d'aujourdhui que je sçais les bonnes intentions de M. Law pour sa patrie, et les desseins qu'il a de mettre le Roi mal avec V. A. R. Il n'y a que huit jours que M. Law nous a menacé publiquement, en presence de plusieurs sujets du Roi mon maître, d'écrire un livre pour convaincre toute la terre que Grande Bretagne étoit dans l'impossibilité de payer ses dettes. Tels sont les discours ordinaires et publiques de M. Law. V. A. R. peut juger quel effet cela peut produire, quand un homme qui prétend étre votre premier ministre tient des tels discours. Il y a long temps que je le scai, mais je n'en ai rien dit à V. A. R. parceque j'étois persuadé qu'elle ne pensoit pas de même; et parceque je regardois ces discours comme les effets de la sotte vanité et de l'yvresse de M. Law, dont, depuis quelque temps, je lui voyois la tête tournée. Ensuite je contai à M. le Duc d'Orléans beaucoup d'autres discours de cette même nature. M. le Duc a écouté tout ce discours avec des convulsions dans son visage. A la fin, il me dit, Mylord, voila véritablement les discours d'un fou. Je lui dis, Monseigneur, je ne dis rien à V. A. R. que je ne disse en présence de M. Law, et que je ne prouve; aprés cela V. A. R. peut juger s'il auroit été étonnant si j'avois veritablement agi de la manière que M. Law a fait accroire à V, A. R. que j'avois agi, mais je me suis gouverné par les égards que j'ai toujours eu pour les intérêts de V. A. R.

M. le Duc d'Orléans me dit à la fin, qu'il étoit très aise de ce que je venois de lui dire; qu'il m'avoit toujours regardé comme son ami, et qu'il avoit eu de la peine à croire que j'eusse voulu nuire à ses opérations. Voila à peu près ce que s'est passé entre M. le Duc d'Orléans et moi sur le chapitre de M. Law. Vous y ferez les réflexions nécessaires. Cela n'a pas besoin de commentaire.'[62]

'Le Régent s'apperçoit si bien des dangers ou Law le précipite, qu'il m'a dit depuis quelques jours, à plusieurs reprises, les choses du monde les plus fortes contre la vanité, la présomption, et l'insolence de cet homme. Il m'a dit, qu'il le connoissoit pour un homme à qui la vanité et l'ambition démesurée avoit tournée la tête; que rien ne pouvoit le satisfaire que d'étre le maître absolu; qu'il avoit une telle présomption de ses propres talens, et un tel mépris pour touts les autres hommes, qu'il étoit impracticable avec tout autre homme; qu'il avoit essayé de le faire travailler avec tout ce qu'il y a d'habilles gens en France, et qu'il n'avoit pu s'accommoder deux jours de suite, avec qui ce soit, étant impatient de tout espèce de contrariété ou contradiction. Il m'a dit qu'il lui avoit lavée la tête de ses discours insolens qui alarmoient tout le monde, de manière qu'il avoit lieu de croire que Law se seroit contenu; mais qu'il voyoit bien que nul frein le pouvoit retenir. Mais, dit le Régent, croyez moi que j'y mettrai si bien ordre qu'il ne sera pas capable de me brouiller avec le Roi, ni de me deviser de mes alliez. Il faut que je m'en serve dans mes finances; mais il ne, sera écouté dans les affaires politiques, et je serai en garde contre les mauvais desseins qu'il peut avoir.

Je veux bien croire que le Régent dit ce qu'il pense, et qu'il le pensoit véritablement dans le moment qu'il m'a parlé; mais,

62. 11 December 1719.

avec tout cela, un grand trésorier tel que Law est premier ministre par tout ou il se trouve en place; et si le système de Law s'établit, nous sommes également perdus, un an plus tot, un an plus tard. Et de plus, croyez moi, nous devons connoitre cette nation ici; nous ne pouvons jamais, avec raison, compter sur leur amitié, que tant que vous serez en état de leur étre un ennemi dangereux, et de leur faire envisager des grands maux que nous pourrions leur faire si elle rompoit avec vous. Sur ce pied la, leur amitié sera asseurée; mais nous nous mecompterons toutes les fois que nous nous fions sur eux en cas de besoin.

Vous auriez reçeu un courier de M. l'Abbé Dubois, par lequel il vous aura dit, que je lui ai dit, jeudi dernier, que je démanderois d'étre rapellé. Ce n'est pas par picque; mais je prévois, par le train que les affaires prennent, je ne serai plus en état de pouvoir rendre aucun service au Roi dans cette cour.'[63]

These endeavours of Lord Stair to render the regent dissatisfied with a minister who, whatever were his designs against Britain, served his prince with fidelity, recoiled on the ambassador's head. The British ministry beginning to entertain the most serious apprehensions of danger from the power and abilities of the comptroller general, and dreading that Lord Stair's measures would have no other effect than to irritate him the more against England, determined to sacrifice that able and accomplished nobleman to their fears. They accused him of preferring to the public good and the king's service, his own humour and resentment; and of attempting to embroil England with France, in order to gratify his private pique against Mr. Law, to whom they now thought it necessary to make all sorts of advances; and, for this purpose, dispatched no less a person than Earl Stanhope, one of the Secretaries of State, to Paris. Lord Stair wrote to Mr. Craggs, 'I shall readily agree with you, that if his Lordship' (Stanhope) 'has gained Mr. Law, and made

---

63. 7th January 1720.

him lay aside his ill will and ill designs against his country, he did very right to make all sorts of advances to him; to give his son a regiment; to engage to bring Lord Banbury[64] into the

64. Charles, fourth Earl of Banbury, whose sister, Lady Catherine Knollys, was the wife of Mr. Law, and whose eldest son and heir- apparent, William Viscount Wallingford, married Miss Law. The editor of the Hardwicke State Papers says in a note, that 'his son,' to whom a regiment was promised, was 'Lord Wallingford, who married Law's daughter.' But this marriage did not take place till 1734, after Mr. Law's death. In 1720, Mr. Law's son was only seventeen years of age, while Lord Wallingford was thirty years old, and an officer in the British service, which renders it more probable he was the person intended. 'To bring Lord Banbury into the House of Lords,' requires a particular explanation. Sir William Knollys, K. G. grandson of Lady Mary Boleyn, sister of Queen Anne Boleyn, the mother of Queen Elizabeth, was created, 13th May 1603, Baron Knollys of Greys; 7th November 1616, Viscount of Wallingford; and 18th August 1626, Earl of Banbury, to him and the heirs male of his body. He died 25th May 1632, in the eighty-eighth year of his age, leaving, by his second wife, Lady Elizabeth Howard, daughter of Thomas, first Earl of Suffolk, two sons, Edward, born 10th April 1627, and Nicholas, born 3rd January 1630-1. Edward, the eldest, second Earl of Banbury, was killed in a sudden quarrel on the roadway between Calais and Gravelines, a minor and unmarried. His brother Nicholas, third Earl of Banbury, sat as a peer in the Convention Parliament 1660, which assembled without writ; a question arose as to his title, but it was not further proceeded in. He was not summoned to the next Parliament 1661, on account of doubts of his legitimacy, the Earl of Banbury being so far advanced in life when the two sons were born of his countess. He presented to the king a petition for a writ of summons, which was referred to the House of Lords. Witnesses were examined before the Committee of Privileges, who, in July 1661, reported that Nicholas, Earl of Banbury, is a legitimate person, being, in the eye of the law, the son of William, Earl of Banbury, and that the house should therefore advise the king to send him a writ

to come to Parliament. But none was sent; and he and his successors stood in the awkward predicament of having a patent for the title, but of being without the writ which would enable them to sit in Parliament, or to be considered as peers. Thus, in commissions of the peace and army, and in other formal proceedings, they were styled Earls of Banbury, and were rated to the capitation tax as such, but were liable to be sued in the ordinary form as commoners. Nicholas, third Earl of Banbury, died 14th March 1673-4; he was twice married, first to Lady Isabella Blount, eldest daughter of Mountjoy Earl of Newport, by whom he had one daughter; secondly to Anne, daughter of William Lord Sherard, by whom he had several children, particularly Charles, fourth Earl of Banbury; Lady Anne Maria, married first to Major Walter Littleton, second son of Sir Edward Littleton of Pillaton Hall, in Staffordshire, baronet, secondly to Captain Philip Lawson, sixth son of Sir John Lawson of Brough in Yorkshire, baronet, both of whom were killed in duels, thirdly to Colonel Harvey; and Lady Catherine, married to Mr. Law. Charles, fourth Earl of Banbury, born 3rd June 1662, had the misfortune of being engaged in a duel with swords, with his brother-in-law Philip Lawson, who received a mortal wound in his side, and died on the spot, 6th December 1692. An indictment for murder being, on this occasion, found against the Earl of Banbury by the name of Charles Knollys, Esq. he petitioned the House of Lords, 14th December 1692, to be tried as a peer; but the House resolved, by a small majority, 17th January 1692-3, that he had not any right to the title of Earl of Banbury. The indictment was removed by certiorari into the Court of King's Bench, where the defendant being arraigned in Trinity Term 1694, he pleaded in abatement of the indictment misnomer, namely, that he is Earl of Banbury, producing the letters patent to the first earl, and setting forth the descents to himself. The Attorney General replied, that the defendant had petitioned the House of Lords to be tried on this indictment by his peers, and that thereupon the House disallowed his peerage, and dismissed the petition. To this replication the defendant demurred, and the Attorney General joined in demurrer. Lord Chief Justice Holt and the other judges held the plea good, being of opinion that the defendant had a title to his honour by legal conveyance; that the House of Lords could no more deprive one of a peerage than they could confer that dignity; that the letters-patent produced by the defendant could not be cancelled without a *scire facias*; and that the legitimacy of his father could not now be questioned. Judgment went for defendant, the indictment was abated, and he remained untried. The House of Lords being offended at this decision, called Lord Chief- Justice Holt and Justice Eyre to the bar in February 1697, and interrogated them as to the reasons thereof; no other answer was received from these great judges than that their judgment, if erroneous, was open to be corrected only by the forms of law, namely, by writ of error. But no such writ was brought, and the judgment of the Court of King's Bench remained un-reversed. The promise to Mr. Law to bring Lord Banbury into the House of Lords was not fulfilled, no writ of summons being issued. He died 28th August 1740, and his successors still retained the designation of Earls of Banbury. Thomas Woods Knollys, seventh Earl of Banbury, dying at Winchester 13th May 1793, was succeeded by his only son, William, eighth Earl of Banbury. His Lordship was an officer in the third regiment of Foot Guards for thirty-six years, rising gradually from the station of ensign in 1778, to that of first major of the regiment, which he held when he quitted it in 1814, having then the rank of lieutenant-general in the army. In his commissions he was designed Viscount Wallingford, and, after his father's death, Earl of Banbury. In 1806 he presented 'to the king's most excellent Majesty, the humble petition of William Earl of Banbury,' entering into a detail of all former proceedings, and concluding thus: 'Your Majesty's petitioner, conceiving that he has made out such a statement as is sufficient to shew that he is the true and lawful heir of the said dignity of Earl of Banbury, so granted to his ancestor, and that he cannot legally divest himself thereof, or write or call himself by any other name or title, respectfully implores that justice and protection to which none of your Majesty's subjects ever appealed in vain, and humbly prays that your Majesty will be pleased to grant him a writ of summons to your Parliament as Earl of Banbury, or to take such other

House of Lords; to sacrifice the king's ambassador to him. If I had thought Mr. Law to be gained, I should very readily have advised to do all these very things, and a great deal more. But if his Lordship has not gained Mr. Law, I am afraid we shall not find our account in Lord Stanhope's supporting him, when he was ready to fall; in making him first minister; and in destroying the personal credit I had with the regent, and recalling me from this court, where my long stay should have enabled me to be better able to judge of their design, and of their ways of working, than a stranger of greater capacity could probably be. A little time will shew who has judged rightest. I do most heartily wish, for the good of my country, that I may be found to have formed a wrong judgment; but I own to you, I have seen nothing yet to make me change my opinion, but, on the contrary, new things every day to confirm me, that Mr. Law's designs, and the views of this court, are just what I represented them to be. You do me great wrong if you say that I advised to break with the regent if he did not agree to part with Mr. Law.

steps as to your Majesty's great wisdom shall seem meet, for the purpose of producing a full investigation and final determination of his case.' This petition was, 22nd May 1806, referred to the Attorney General, and afterwards, 5th February 1808, referred, with the Attorney General's opinion, to the House of Lords, by whom it was resolved and adjudged, 15th March 1813, that the petitioner is not entitled to the title, dignity, and honour of Earl of Banbury. A strong protest, however, drawn up by Lord Erskine, signed by his Lordship, the Royal Dukes of Kent, Sussex, and Gloucester, the Marquis of Hastings, Earl Nelson, Lords Ponsonby, Dundas, Ashburton, and Hood, was entered on the journals against this resolution. The Earl of Banbury consequently dropped that title, is now designed William Knollys, and ranks as general in the army from 12th August 1819. Journals of the House of Lords; State Trials; Dugdale, ii. 412; Salkeld, ii. 509; Dormant and Extinct Baronage of England, by T. C. Banks, iii. 44.

You will find no such thing in my letters. You will find there that I thought it was useful to shake Mr. Law's credit with his master, to make his master jealous of Mr. Law's ambition, and apprehensive of the dangers his presumption might lead him into; and that I thought it was fit to stand in his way as much as it was possible, to hinder him to gain an absolute power over the regent's mind, and to obstruct his becoming first minister. I thought it was fit to make Mr. Law lose temper, and to make him act in passion and rage. I had not succeeded in these views when Lord Stanhope arrived, and thought fit to demolish me and all my works at once.

You will find, besides, in my letters, that I advised with more warmth than possibly became a man of so little weight as I am, to think of speedy ways to put the payment of the public debts into a method, as the only sure way to avert the dangers which I took to be imminent, and the only way to procure a good understanding between our court and that of France.

But you do me greater wrong when you say, that the representations I made of the dangers we were in, proceeded only from my resentment against particular persons. These are cruel insinuations to be made to one's master and their country.' – 'As to Mr. Law I have no ill will to him but as I take him to be a dangerous enemy to my country. I am afraid time will but too plainly shew that I have judged right in that matter.

As to my revocation; if it was possible that I should have a mind to stay in this country, you have made it impracticable. You have taken all effectual ways to be thought of to destroy the personal credit I had with the regent. You have made it plain to him that I have no credit with the king; that is to say, with his ministers. Lord Stanhope has declared to Mr. Law that I shall be recalled, so that is no longer a question; you are under the necessity of sending another minister to this court.'[65]

---

65. 14th February 1720.

'I will agree with you that the king was in the right not to put things upon that issue with the regent, that he would have peace and friendship with him if he would sacrifice Law, but war with him if he would not. Now, I must beg pardon to say two things; first, that I never did put things upon that issue; and, in the next place, that there was no need of putting things upon that issue.

You will find in my letters that I represented to the Duke of Orléans that Law, by his vanity and presumption, was leading him into great dangers and inconveniences both at home and abroad; that Law, by going too fast, and by taking arbitrary measures, was in a way to ruin his highness's credit with the nation, and to overturn the whole system of the finances; and that, at the same time, Law was, by his discourse and his conduct, doing every thing that lay in his power to destroy the good understanding between the king and the regent, and between the regent and the rest of his allies; and I bade the regent beware how he trusted the reins of his chariot to that Phaeton Law, because he would overturn it. The answer the regent made me to these representations was, that he knew vanity and ambition had turned his head, but that he, the regent, would take care to keep a hand over him, and to contain him within bounds in the management of the finances; that he should have nothing to say in public affairs; that if he presumed to meddle, the regent would not listen to him; and that I might be well assured that it should not be in his power to create an ill understanding between him and the king.

I believe nobody can fairly say that there is any thing in these representations which imported that the king would quarrel with the regent if he did not lay Law aside. Nor can they say that there is any thing in the regent's answer which imports that he took what I said in that sense. On this foot things stood. I spoke very freely to the regent what I had to say on the subject of Mr. Law, and his royal highness received what I said in a very friendly manner.

When Lord Stanhope arrived, he thought fit to acknowledge Mr. Law as first minister, and to consider him as a much greater man than Cardinal Richelieu or Cardinal Mazarine had been; to tell the regent that the king was very well satisfied with Mr. Law, and did not in any manner complain of him; that what I had said was entirely out of my own head, and without, and even contrary to, orders; and that, for so doing, I should be recalled. Since that time Mr. Law has acted as first minister; and I have had no intercourse with the regent but in formal audiences, to deliver such messages as I received from court, and to receive short and formal answers. In what manner Mr. Law has acted as first minister I may save the trouble of telling you; you have seen and felt it.

My dear Craggs, take my word for it Mr. Law's plan is formed to destroy the king and his government, and our nation, and he will certainly bring his master into it; nor is there any other way to divert him from that design but by shewing his master that it is dangerous for him to attack us. There is nothing but an appearance of strength and firmness on our side, or the miscarriage of Law's system on this side, can save us from a war with France; and no personal credit that anybody may flatter themselves they have with the Duke of Orléans, will signify any thing to divert it. Your letter about Gibraltar is very well writ, and it was very right to write it; but I will give you my word for it, it will have no manner of weight here if Law's system takes place. If they can bully the ministry, or make a party in England, we must part with Gibraltar; and when we have parted with it, we shall be every way as little secure of peace as we are at present, and, on many accounts, less able to support a war.'[66]

66. 12th March 1720.

'I am glad you do not apprehend that Mr. Law is in a condition to do us any great hurt, by what he gets by the rise of our South Sea stock. Though 1 know that Law will brag, yet I own to you I did apprehend that he had gained considerably, and that he might be able to do us a good deal of mischief by withdrawing a very great sum himself, and by tempting other foreigners to follow his example. I suppose you know that the great sums Mr. Law pretends to have in our stocks were bought in Holland.

It seems to me to be a dangerous thing in such a country as ours, where things are so very uncertain and fluctuating, to have foreigners masters of such vast sums of money as they must needs have at present, by the rise of our stocks. That is a terrible handle to hurt us by, in the hands of such a man as Law.

I am afraid our people in England, think too neglectfully of Mr. Law's schemes. I own to you, that as this kingdom is disposed, there is great odds to be laid that it will miscarry; but it is not impossible, far from it, that it may hold long enough to do us a good deal of mischief. Another thing, I dare be bold to say, it cannot succeed without undoing us; and if Mr. Law can compass our ruin, I think he is in a fair way to carry through his project in France. I know Mr. Law himself thinks so too; and that being the case, we may be very sure he will do us all the mischief in his power. You cannot think that power is small, considering the absolute authority he has acquired over the regent. That being so, you will agree with me that we cannot be too attentive to discover, prevent, and defeat the designs he may form against us. His designs are no trifling ones; they strike at the root.'[67]

'I see plainly that I shall not be able to see the king in England. It is a great while since Mr. Law told his friends here that I should not be allowed to have the honour of seeing the

67. 30th April 1720.

king. It is pretty hard to digest, I own, if, after serving the king very faithfully, very zealously, and with some success, I should have the mortification not so much as to have my master's good countenance.'[68]

The Earl of Stair returned to England immediately afterwards, when his successor, Sir Robert Sutton, arrived in Paris; and was not employed in any civil or military capacity for upwards of twenty years. During that time he resided at Newliston, living in a very frugal manner, having put his estate into the hands of trustees, in order to pay off the debts contracted during this embassy, one of the most splendid and magnificent ever known, as government refused to discharge them. The Comptroller General thus beheld these attempts to shake his power serve no other purpose than to establish it the more firmly, and triumphed over one of the ablest and most deserving ministers Britain ever sent abroad.[69]

At this high pinnacle, idolized by the French, dreaded by the other European states, and courted by the kingdom that had passed sentence of death upon him, we will leave Mr. Law for a while, and go on with the history of the System.

The credit of the Bank and of the India Company had arrived at its acme in November 1719, shares of the latter selling for more than 10,000 livres each; and such was the abundance of money in the former, that the directors agreed to lend any sum on proper security, at an annual interest of only two percent. To increase the good humour and confidence of the public, when the annual rent of the loan of 100 millions from the company to the king was reduced one percent, by which his Majesty made a saving of one million of livres per year, the regent, at the request of that body, abolished the taxes on oil, tallow, and paper, amounting to 1,063,000 livres annually,

68. 12th June 1720.

69. Douglas' Peerage, ii. 530.

and he moreover remitted arrears of duties due to the king, to the extent of 52,178,546 livres. The Company likewise, of their own accord, suppressed the tax of twenty-four deniers in the livre on fish, part of the general farms assigned to them, a tax that used to produce 200,000 livres per year; actions that could not fail to be very acceptable to the people, who became more than ever enamoured of the System.[70]

In the midst of this general delirium, however, a constant drain of specie from the bank was observable. This was occasioned by the conduct of several of the original proprietors of the India Company, who, astonished at their exorbitant gains, could think of nothing but converting their shares into gold and silver, which they either hoarded up, or remitted abroad; insomuch that it was computed no less than 500 millions of livres, the property of persons of that description, had been sent out of France.[71] This circumstance, united to the

70. Examen, i. 315. Hist. Syst. ii. 5.

71. Vernesobre de Laurieu, a Prussian of mean origin, whom Mr. Law had patronised, and appointed one of the cashiers of the royal bank, having found means to remit near forty millions of livres to England, Holland, and Germany, disappeared at once, to the no small consternation of the India Company. Returning to his native country, his prodigious wealth occasioned him, although no better than an infamous robber, to be received with open arms by persons of the highest distinction in Prussia, where he was advanced to the first places in the financial department, and honoured with the order of the Black Eagle. One M. le Cevennois having gained several millions by the first operations of the system, carried them into England, where he increased his wealth by speculating in the South Sea funds. Bourdon and La Richardiere, two famous stockjobbers, remitted hundreds of thousands of louis d'or to England, along with a great quantity of diamonds, and several cargoes of brandy, a commodity that they had engrossed. One Vermalet having gained more than a million of livres, converted them into specie, and carried the whole to

prodigious quantity of gold and silver made into plate for the rich *Mississippians*, was the cause that there scarcely remained in the kingdom a sufficiency of specie for ordinary circulation. With the view of averting the danger with which these practices threatened the system, and also of guarding against a run upon the bank, which it was natural to apprehend would infallibly take place when the state creditors were paid off, as it was now proposed to discharge their demands, several edicts were issued during the months of January, February, and March, 1720. By these, payments in specie were restricted to small sums, (so low as 100 livres in gold, and 10 livres in silver;) the standard of the coin was kept in a continual state of fluctuation; bank notes were declared to remain always invariable, and even to be current at five (and in some cases ten) percent above the specie; all rents, taxes, and customs were ordered to be paid in notes; and plate was prohibited to be made without the royal licence. These, and other similar edicts now published, served the double purpose of increasing the profits of the mint to the India Company, and throwing gold and silver out of circulation; so that it would appear Mr. Law now began to entertain the idea of abolishing the use of specie altogether, especially since permission was given to every one to export coin and the metals of which it was made. But what crowned all was the famous edict of the 27th February 1720, prohibiting individuals, and secular or religious communities, (some privileged officers excepted,) from having in their possession more than 500 livres in specie, under pain of a heavy fine, and confiscation of the sums found; an edict which could not fail to produce the most disagreeable consequences upon the peace of families, rendering the nearest relations suspicious of each other, and parents apprehensive of their children turning informers. Several were convicted of,

---

Holland, in a cart loaded with hay and straw, driven by himself. Hist. Syst. i, 175, 187, ii. 46, iv. 38, 42.

and punished for, contravening this edict, among others, a director of the India Company; but it had in the main so much effect, as to occasion the people to run in crowds to the bank, to exchange their specie for paper, and to think themselves happy when this was accomplished. The eagerness manifested to get near the tellers for that purpose induced one to say to some of these importunate persons, 'Do not be afraid, gentlemen, that your money will be suffered to remain on your hands; I will engage that all shall be taken from you.' It was said that above 300 millions of livres were paid in coin into the bank between the 27th February and 1st April 1720; a great sum, but yet little more than one-fifth of the computed specie of the kingdom; for several individuals, who could not be persuaded that paper was of equal value with gold and silver, hoarded up, without intermission, all these precious metals they could procure, notwithstanding the penalties denounced by the before-mentioned edict, which was followed by another of the 11th of March, forbidding any payment whatever to be made in specie.[72]

On the 23rd of February 1720, the royal bank was incorporated with the Company of the Indies, the king remaining guarantee of the bank notes, of which none were, after that date, to be fabricated, except in virtue of edicts of council. His Majesty moreover gave up to the company all the profits made by the bank since he had taken it into his hands in December 1718; and the public entertaining the idea that these profits were immense, this contributed to raise higher than ever the reputation of the India company's opulence. For some time previous and subsequent to this incorporation, the fabrication of bank notes went on at so great a rate, that upwards of 2000 millions were struck off between the 29th December 1719 and 1st May 1720; and during this period, it

72. Stewart, ii. 265. Examen, i. 319, 344. Mem. Reg. ii. 300.

appears that a final conclusion was put to the reimbursement of the national creditors by these notes, in consequence whereof the government securities granted to them were withdrawn and cancelled.[73]

The respectable author of the *Inquiry into the Principles of Political Economy* supposes that it now was the intention of the regent to dispose of as many of the shares he already possessed, and of those which the company were bound to sell to his Royal Highness, (he asserts, at the rate of 5000 livres each,) as would retire the amount of the national debt already discharged, and then to destroy the bank notes so withdrawn. The whole public debts of France would consequently be converted into shares of the India company, who would have become responsible to the respective proprietors for the dividend on the shares thus disposed of, and to the regent for that on those which might have remained in his possession. If we suppose the price of shares during so great an operation not to fall below 10,000 livres each, the amount of the whole national debt could be withdrawn by the sale of 200,000 shares. In that case the regent would still have 200,000 shares left in his hands; and the dividend on these, at 200 livres each, amounting to forty millions, being deducted from the forty-eight millions payable annually by the king as the interest of the loan from the company, leaves a remainder of eight millions, all that his Majesty would have to pay, instead of eighty millions as at first. This sum of eight millions might even have been altogether extinguished, if either the price of shares or the quantum of dividend had increased, or the rate of interest been sunk to a degree sufficient to answer that purpose.[74]

The assertion that the company was bound to sell the regent 300,000 actions, at 5000 livres each, seems to be unfounded,

73. Examen, i. 340.

74. Stewart, ii. 267.

no such agreement appearing among the edicts of council.[75] It must be allowed, however, that the above-mentioned plan was both probable and practicable; since by selling the shares of the company, and destroying the paper received for them, no notes except such as had been issued for value by the bank would have remained in circulation. The bank consequently having it in their power to answer all demands, their credit must have been completely established and confirmed. Whether the regent entertained any such design is, however, merely conjectural; for the time now approached with hasty strides, when the public credit of France, high as it had been raised, was at once to give way, involve many in widely extended ruin, and crush its author, who merited a better fate. The following steps led to this strange and unexpected event.

The envy that generally is the attendant on persons raised to high offices of state, Mr. Law could not fail to have the misfortune of experiencing; and, in his case, it was heightened to a very inveterate degree, from the circumstance of his being a foreigner. He was hated by almost all the ministry, and obnoxious to the old retainers of the court. Cardinal Dubois in particular, formerly the regent's tutor, a man not to be equaled in wickedness and profligacy, could not, without pain, observe his wonted influence over the mind of his old pupil quite destroyed by the superior attractions of the Comptroller General, who, he had reason to suspect, was determined to have him exiled from court. This made him attempt all methods to injure Mr. Law in the opinion of the regent, in which he

75. It appears that in June 1720, the Company was in possession of 300,000 actions; and that the regent had 100,000 shares belonging to him. When the Bank was incorporated with the Company of the Indies, it was agreed by them to purchase these 100,000 shares at the rate of 9000 livres each, payable by installments; an agreement the subsequent calamities prevented from being completed. Examen, i. 343.

was joined by several of his colleagues; while, at the same time, the great men of the court, enriched beyond their utmost hopes, slackened in their zeal for, and turned cool towards the interests of, the prime minister. The farmers general, irritated by the loss they sustained by taking the great farms into their hands, combined against Mr. Law; and the parliament of Paris, who reckoned that gentleman their most bitter enemy, leagued themselves with these rich and powerful financiers. The united efforts of such a number of antagonists appear to have made a deep impression on the regent, from the following passages in a letter of Lord Stair, dated 12th March 1720:

'You may depend upon it, that Law is mightily shaken in his master's good opinion, who, within these few days past, has used him most cruelly to his face, and calling him all the names that can be thought of, knave and madman, etc. He told him he did not know what hindered him to send him to the Bastile, and that there was never one sent thither deserved it half so well. This scene happened in the presence of Le Blanc, (the Secretary at War.) The Duke of Orléans was upon the close stool when Law came in. The Duke was in such a passion that he ran to Law with his breeches about his heels, and made him the compliment above mentioned.'[76] It however appears by

76. From the conclusion of this letter we learn, that the cares of his station, the pressure of business, or the adulation so lavishly bestowed on him, or perhaps all these causes combined, had begun to affect the minister's brain. 'Law's head is so heated that he does not sleep at nights, and has formal fits of frenzy. He gets out of bed almost every night, and runs stark staring mad about the room, making a terrible noise, sometimes singing and dancing; at other times swearing, staring, and stamping, quite out of himself. Some nights ago, his wife, who had come into the room upon the noise he made, was forced to ring the bell for people to come to her assistance. The officer of Law's guard was the first that came, and found Law in his shirt, who had set two chairs in the middle of the

other letters from his Lordship, of a later date, that Mr. Law soon regained a great share of the regent's confidence, though his Highness could not erase from his mind the impression he had received from the reiterated unfavourable reports made by his enemies. But an opportunity soon afterwards occurred, and was eagerly embraced by them, of engaging the Duke in a scheme which completely ruined the great designs of the Comptroller General, by putting an end to his plans of public credit and national affluence.[77]

It has been before mentioned, that at the first of May 1720, bank notes had been fabricated to the amount of above 2600 millions of livres. The specie in the kingdom was estimated at the rate of sixty-five livres to the marc, at 1300 millions. Cardinal Dubois, M. d'Argenson, and others of the ministry, now represented to the regent that it was become absolutely necessary to form an equal proportion between the notes and the coin, by either raising the denomination of the latter to 130 livres the marc, by which the 1300 millions of specie would have been augmented to 2600 millions of specie; or reducing the value of the notes one half, that is, to 1300 millions. This extraordinary point was debated in council; some of the members, among whom was the Comptroller General, contended strenuously for letting matters stand as they were; or if it was judged necessary to adopt one of the alternatives, they proposed to raise the denomination of the specie, a measure that had frequently been practised before. The majority of the council, however, who bore no good will to Mr. Law, favouring the proposition for lowering the value of the paper, it was at last, after a profound deliberation, determined to issue an edict

room, and was dancing round them, quite out of his wits. This scene the officer of the guard told Le Blanc, from whom it came to me by a very sure conveyance.' Hardwicke State Papers.

77. Massillon, 147. Richelieu, iii. 45.

for that purpose.[78]

Accordingly, on the 21st of May 1720, an edict was published, stating, that the king having judged that the general interests of his subjects required that the price, or nominal value of the India company's actions, and of bank notes, should be lessened, for maintaining a just proportion between them and the coin and other commodities of the kingdom; his Majesty ordered that the shares of the company should be reduced, beginning from the day of the publication of the present edict, to 8000 livres; on the 1st of July to 7500 livres; on the 1st of August to 7000 livres; and so on by 500 livres per month till the 1st of December, when they were to remain fixed at 5000 livres. That the bank notes should also be reduced, so as they should be received in payments from that date at the following rates; *viz* those of 10,000 livres for 8000 livres, those of 1000 livres for 800, of 100 for 80, and of 10 for 8. That on the 1st of July these notes should be further reduced, those of 10,000 livres to 7500 livres, and so on at the rate of 500 livres per month, the lesser notes being reduced in the like proportion, till the 1st of December, when it was declared that the bank notes should remain fixed, those of 10,000 livres at 5000 livres, those of 1000 at 500, those of 100 at 50, and those of 10 at 5 livres.[79]

That this unjustifiable and fatal step was taken in opposition to the advice of the Comptroller General, is asserted upon the authority of his nephew, M. Law de Lauriston, who says, 'On se décida, malgré l'avis de M, Law, et sur son rapport cependant, puisqu'il étoit Controleur Général des Finances, mais peu écouté, de lancer l'arrêt,' etc. Indeed, it seems hardly credible, that one so intimately conversant in the principles of public credit as Mr. Law was could approve of a proceeding

78. Stewart, ii. 268.

79. Hist. Syst. iii. 149. Recherches et Considérations sur les Finances de France, vi. 336.

diametrically opposite to them. Several, who cannot be supposed to be biased by sinister motives, unite in declaring that the Comptroller General had no hand in the framing of that fatal edict, which they allege was the work of M. d'Argenson. The author of the History of the System says, in direct terms, that Mr. Law strongly opposed the issuing of the edict, contending, that the least symptom of reduction would for ever put an end to all confidence and credit; and some go so far as to maintain, on the authority of a letter from a duke and peer of France to an English nobleman, that the other European States, entertaining serious apprehensions that, in the event of the system's being attended with success, the consequent increase of the power and wealth of France would prove prejudicial to their interests, the ministers of the Quadruple Alliance concerted the mode of occasioning the miscarriage of that project, and suggested it to the enemies of Mr. Law.[80]

Be the cause as it may, the edict was published; and the consequences of this infraction of the royal engagement, which solemnly promised, that whatever alterations should take place on the coin, the bank notes should always remain invariable, and be paid in full, were such as might have been expected. From that moment

Omnia fatis
In pejus ruere, ac retro sublapsa referri,

the whole paper fabric fell to the ground, the notes lost all credit, none would meddle with them; and the avenues of the bank being blocked up by soldiers, there was no possibility of getting near the tellers, so that the day following, 22nd of May,

80. Hist. Syst. ii. 196, iii. 146. Examen, i. 360. Réfl. Polit. i. 235. Le secrèt du système de M. Law devoilé, en deux lettres écrites par un Duc et Pair de France, à un Milord Anglois. La Haye, 1721.

any one might have starved with 100 millions of paper money in his pocket.[81]

The consternation with which all ranks were struck on the publication of this fatal edict being quickly converted into rage, it became necessary to station a number of troops in different quarters of Paris, to bridle the fury of the mob, from whose outrageous disposition a second tragedy of St. Bartholomew was dreaded. Disorder and confusion reigned everywhere; seditious and inflammatory libels were posted up and distributed; and the life of the regent himself was threatened. But that Prince, among whose failings want of courage certainly never could be reckoned, disregarding these menaces, continued to give public audience every day in the Palais Royal.[82]

In this emergency, the parliament of Paris called an extraordinary meeting to deliberate upon the situation of

81. Stewart, ii. 268.

82. In this season of calamity, the French, with their characteristic levity, could not refrain from sporting with their own misfortunes in epigrams and other *jeux d'esprit*. The following are selected from an infinity of productions of that nature:

Lundi j'achetai des actions;
Mardi je gagnai des millions;
Mercredi j'arrangeai mon ménage;
Jeudi je pris un équipage;
Vendredi je m'en fus au bal;
Et Samedi a l'Hopital.

To the Abbé (afterwards Cardinal) de Tencin, who had the principal hand in Mr. Law's conversion, for which he was rewarded with the Bishopric of Grenoble:

Foin de ton zèle séraphique,
Malheureux Abbé de Tencin!
Depuis que Laws est cath clique,
Tout le royaume est capuçin.

affairs; and the result of this meeting was sending a deputation, composed of their principal members, to the regent, to demand the revocation of the edict of the 21st of May. Upon their representation, this was accordingly done by another edict, dated 27th of May, establishing the paper at its former denomination. But all confidence being now gone, this edict had no other effect than to increase the mischief, by throwing again into the channel of commerce notes universally discredited, with which knavish persons paid and ruined their lawful creditors.[83] To render matters worse, payment was the same day stopped at the bank, commissaries being sent to seal up the repositories, and to examine the account books. This was done under pretext of inquiring into frauds alleged to have been committed by the clerks, but in reality to prevent the specie from being paid away in exchange for notes; and this procedure did not fail to increase the disorder and confusion of affairs.[84]

The distress of the people may easily be conceived to have been extreme, when it is considered, that at the time the bank thus stopped payment, no less than 2,235,085,590 livres of notes were in circulation.[85] It now became necessary to issue an edict, permitting all persons to have in their possession whatever sums in specie they thought proper, and a quantity of silver was sent to the commissaries of each section of Paris,

---

83. The President de Novion having, some months preceding, sold an estate to Mr. Law for 400,000 livres in gold, and having reserved a right of redemption within a stated period, his son, availing himself of that clause, at this juncture repaid the purchaser with notes.

84. Richelieu, iii. 28. Hist. Syst. ii. 91, iii. 159. Stewart, ii. 270. Mem. Reg. iii. 4.

85. The total amount of notes fabricated by this time was, as has been before stated, 2,696,400,000 livres, and of them 461,316,410 livres remained on the 27th of May in the bank, which was also possessed of 336,011,050 livres in specie. Stewart, ii. 271.

to give in change for small notes to those who had the most pressing occasion for supply. On the 10th of June, the bank was opened for the payment of notes of 10 livres; on the 11th it was announced that the notes of 100 livres were to be changed there into small notes, only one to be brought by each person coming for that purpose; and the 12th and 13th were appointed for the payments of notes of 10 livres. This being the only place where specie could be procured, it is no wonder that the confluence of people there should be immense; and, accordingly, scarcely a day passed without some being suffocated or crushed to death in the crowd. On the 9th of July, an enormous throng of people assembled at the entrance of the bank on the side of the Mazarin Gardens. The guards took care that a very small number should be admitted; and the gate being immediately shut, those on the outside began to be very clamorous, and to throw stones at the door and into the gardens, which was returned from within; and one of the soldiers firing his piece through the key hole, killed a coachman, and wounded a citizen in the shoulder. At last the gate was opened; but the guards being ranged in the inside with fixed bayonets, few chose to venture within their reach, and those who did so paid dear for their temerity, several being wounded, and one run through the body. The 17th of July being appointed for the payment of notes of 100 livres, so extraordinary a concourse assembled, and their struggles were such, that it is said no less than twenty persons were suffocated. This occasioned a dreadful ferment among the Parisians, which was quelled with great difficulty by the prudent conduct of M. le Blanc, Secretary at War.[86]

It may well be supposed that the notes would be retired but very slowly in this manner; therefore, in order to give vent to the deluge of paper that overwhelmed the nation, twenty-

86. Examen, ii. 25. Richelieu, iii. 220. Duclos, ii. 3. Mem. Reg. iii. 7. Stewart, ii. 270.

five millions of perpetual annuities, at the rate of forty years purchase, and four millions of annuities on lives, at twenty-five years purchase, were constituted in June 1720. In July following, books of accounts current and transfers, to the extent of 600 millions, were opened at the bank, and in August, eight millions more of perpetual annuities, at the rate of fifty years purchase, were issued. By these methods, it was expected that upwards of 2000 millions of notes would be retired, and the notes so retired were directed to be burnt; but notwithstanding the eager desire of the people to get rid of their paper money, the unfavourable nature of the terms made several hesitate. It was therefore found necessary, on the 15th of August, to publish an edict, declaring that the notes of 10,000 and 1000 livres should have no currency, except for the purchase of annuities and bank accounts, or for the supplemental payments directed to be made on the actions; and by a subsequent edict, all payments whatever in notes were prohibited after the 1st of November 1720. The consequence was, that many having neglected the opportunities of funding their bank notes within the limited time, in hopes they would again recover their credit, or that better terms might be obtained, great sums of these notes were irreparably lost, remaining useless at this day in the possession of individuals.[87]

---

87. Stewart, ii. 271. A remarkable proof of this occurred on the 6th of September 1790, shortly after the Constituent Assembly of France had issued assignats, which, it is almost unnecessary to mention, were notes secured on landed property belonging to the public. A person was observed in the gardens of the Thuilleries, with a crowd about him, examining some papers. These papers turned out to be a parcel of Law's bank notes, amounting to upwards of 100,000 livres, which, it was imagined, had been given him by some royalist to distribute to the multitude, in order to prejudice them against the assignats. This the man denied, affirming that they had been in his possession several years.

With regard to the shares of the India company, it was, by edict of the 3rd of June 1720, ordered that the 100,000 shares belonging to the king, and 300,000 that were in the company's hands, should be committed to the flames, and that 200,000 new shares should be made, and given to those individuals who brought back their old shares, they either making a supplemental payment of 3000 livres on each, or getting two new shares in return for every three they brought back. The dividend on each share was fixed at 360 livres, and the privileges of the company were, at the same time, increased and extended; it being stated that their affairs were in a flourishing situation, their books kept in exact order, the produce of the farms augmented, and that 105 ships with valuable cargoes, not reckoning a number of brigantines and frigates, had sailed, or were on the point of sailing, to their settlements. Soon afterwards, 50,000 new shares were ordered to be made, making in all 250,000 shares; and on the 24th October 1720, an edict appeared, directing a list of all the original proprietors of shares of the India company to be made out. Such as still possessed the full number for which they had subscribed, were ordered to bring them back, to remain in deposit with the company; and those who had sold either the whole or part of their shares, were required to complete the number originally belonging to them, by purchasing from the company the shares in which they were deficient, at the rate of 13,500 livres each.[88]

This edict could not fail to occasion a considerable degree of alarm among the old stockjobbers, many of whom prepared immediately to leave France; so that it was found necessary, on the 29th of October, to prohibit, under pain of death, any person from departing out of the kingdom without express permission from the regent. Several were arrested on the frontiers, in Franche Comte, and in the vicinity of Calais,

88. Mem, Reg. iii. 58.

having large sums in their possession; and the houses of some of the original proprietors being searched, many discoveries were made. In one lodging 20,000 louis d'or in specie were found concealed; and jewels to the value of two millions having been discovered in the house of M. du Pin, secretary to the king, he was sent to the Bastile, notwithstanding his protestations that it ought not to be imputed as a crime to have become rich by the methods established by the Court. The regent, Mr. Law, and many of the most considerable proprietors of shares, did not omit paying ready obedience to the edict, depositing all the actions belonging to them in the office appointed for that purpose; and even, of their own accord, giving up to the company a large proportion of what each possessed. Soon afterwards the great farms, the management and profits of the mint, and the administration of the whole royal revenues, were taken out of the hands of the India company, who thus became reduced to a mere trading body.[89]

These various operations concluded, the total amount of the public debts was found to extend, at the first of January 1721, to 2,289,762,849 livres, besides 125,024 shares of the India company, valued by the proprietors at 899,638,855 livres, making altogether the vast sum of 3,189,401,705 livres. The interest of the former, at two and one-half percent for perpetual annuities, and four percent for annuities on lives, amounted to 54,579,735 livres, while the dividend on the latter, at the rate of 360 livres each share, came to the sum of 45,008,640 livres, extending in whole to 99,588,375 livres of annual rents.[90]

The ministry finding it impossible for the nation to sustain, for any length of time, so heavy a charge, resolved to establish a Commission or *Visa*, to take an account of the claims of the state creditors; and this was accordingly done, by edict of

89. Mem. Reg. iii. 66, 70.

90. Examen, ii. 143.

council dated 26th January 1721. By this edict all persons of that description were directed to transmit to the *Visa* two papers, one entitled *Bordereau*, containing their name, quality, and place of residence, together with the date, number, and amount of their claims on government. In the second paper, or declaration, were to be stated the titles by which they possessed, and the sums respectively paid for these effects. The commissioners were directed to arrange into five classes the proprietors of government securities, and of shares of the India company. The first four classes were composed of those who had acquired them by the money paid by the king when he discharged the old creditors of the state, by the sale of heritable and moveable property, and by the disposal of merchandise or other effects, respectively; while the fifth and last class comprehended all who could give no fair or satisfactory account of the origin of their acquisitions. Deductions at different rates, proportioned to the favourable or unfavourable circumstances attending the claims of the various public creditors, were ordered to be made from the demands of the first four classes, provided they amounted to more than 500 livres; for all claimants whose demands did not exceed that sum, (no less than 251,590 in number,) were directed to be paid in full. The property belonging to the fifth class was, by the edict, ordered to be totally annihilated, whatever the amount might be; and this clause occasioned many shares of the India company to fall so low, that actions which had cost 13,500 livres were now sold for a single louis d'or.[91]

The *Visa* appointed to settle this complicated and difficult liquidation consisted of fifty boards, composed of Masters of Requests and Counsellors of the Great Council, who employed under them no less than 800 clerks; and in order to assist the commissioners in their operations, copies of all contracts for the

91. Examen, ii. 168. Mem. Reg. iii. 133. Hist. Syst. iv. 68. Histoire de France par Fantin, i. 345.

transfer of property, entered into before notaries, between 1st July 1719 and 31st December 1720, were directed to be made out. The effects carried to the *Visa*, by 511,009 individuals, amounted, as stated by the proprietors, to 2,222,597,491 livres in contracts for annuities on lives, perpetual annuities, etc. and this sum the commissioners reduced to 1,676,5015831 livres, the interest of which may be computed at forty-eight millions per year, partly consisting in life annuities, and, therefore, continually diminishing. The shares of the India company were in like manner reduced from 125,024, with a dividend of 360 livres per annum each, to only 55,316, (afterwards increased to 56,000,) each having a dividend of 100 livres the first year, and 150 livres every subsequent year, exclusive of their proportion of the profits of the trade. Thus, in consequence of these arbitrary proceedings, the annual interest payable by the king was diminished to about fifty-six millions of livres, by which his Majesty was a gainer of upwards of forty millions per year, and many of the public creditors were reduced to the utmost misery and distress.[92]

---

92. Examen, ii. passim. Mem. Reg. iii. 307. The expense of the *Visa*, paid by Government, in pursuance of an edict of council, amounted to 9,045,874 livres, 11s. and 9d. The Sieur de Talhouet, Master of Requests, the Abbé Clement, and the Sieurs Daude and Gailly, four persons employed in this business, being convicted of stealing 946 shares of the India company, were condemned to suffer death; but the sentence of the first two was commuted to perpetual imprisonment, and the last two were sent to the galleys for life.

According to Sir James Stewart, the national debt amounted, at the conclusion of the System, to 1,999,072,540 livres. But he only reckons as such the 100 millions due from the king to the India company, and the balance of notes issued by the bank, after deduction of the paper and specie remaining therein, without taking any notice of the shares of the company in the hands of the public. In stating the proceedings

Such were the consequences of the fatal edict of the 21st of May, a piece of folly hardly to be equaled in the annals of any nation, and not easy to be accounted for on any other supposition, than as a contrivance of the French ministry to free themselves from a formidable rival, to accomplish which object they did not hesitate to bring the kingdom to the brink of destruction. But it is by no means so easy to account for the regent's giving his consent to a decree that, besides being a breach of public faith, was an experiment full of danger, by which neither himself nor any other could possibly be benefited. Had no such step been taken, and his Highness allowed the System to go on in the way supposed to have been at first intended, it is not unreasonable to imagine that, infatuated as the people were to acquire shares of the India company, the sums paid to the national creditors would have been retired with the sale of less than 200,000, consequently the public would then have had about 400,000 shares in their hands. The company could, in this case, easily have made good their engagement to pay a dividend of 200 livres on each of these shares, as we have seen that, on a very moderate computation, they enjoyed an annual revenue of above eighty millions, administered by themselves, and capable of great increase. By destroying the notes so retired, none would have remained in circulation except such as had been issued for value by the bank, which could thus have answered all demands

---

and result of the *Visa*, M. du Verney, who, although strongly prejudiced against Mr. Law, explains the whole operations of the System so fully and clearly, and with so much order and distinctness, in his 'Examen du livre intitulé Réflexions Politiques sur les Finances et le Commerce,' as to give very high ideas of his talents and knowledge of the subject, is followed. It is, however, not a little remarkable, that he takes no notice of the specie remaining in the bank when it stopped payment, extending, according to Sir James Stewart, to 336 millions of livres; nor does it clearly appear how this large sum was brought to account.

made upon it. The company being thereby relieved from every apprehension of suffering by a run upon them, would have had leisure to direct their attention to the improvement, by all possible means, of the home revenue, the culture of the colonies, and the extension of their commerce. In this case, what might not have been expected from the exertions of a body of men, possessed of almost unlimited credit, whose funds were immense, who had in their hands the whole foreign trade and possessions, and all the public revenues of the kingdom, and who, moreover, enjoyed the declared protection of government, and the implicit confidence of the people?

The opinion that the System was a monstrous and impracticable monopoly appears to have been taken up without sufficient grounds. All preceding attempts to establish a flourishing trade to the Indies had failed of success, from deficiency of funds in the parties concerned, so that it was far from being an improper step to endeavour to settle the commerce to these places on a solid and extensive basis, the more especially as the exclusive privilege of trading thereto was granted to the company only for a limited period. With regard to taking the great farms out of the hands of the farmers general, it is apprehended that the propriety of that transfer will not be disputed, when the enormous profits made by those extravagant and luxurious financiers, and their unwarrantable exactions, are considered; while, on the other hand, the superior advantage of assuming these farms into the hands of a company, in which no person that could command a moderate sum was excluded from holding a share, is evident. By consolidating into one channel every branch of the public revenue, all unnecessary charges of collection and management were avoided, and, consequently, the taxes must be levied, and their amounts remitted, at the cheapest rate possible. At least it must be acknowledged that the idea was truly great; and Mr. Law's being able to carry matters to the length he did will appear astonishing indeed, when we consider what reception would in this country await a similar attempt to unite the Public Revenues, the Mint, the Banks, the East India and other privileged companies, into the hands of one great association. The very low price at which the shares of the India Company were originally fixed must, however, be allowed to have been a capital error, though perhaps in some measure necessary, to raise the *billets d'état* from the discredit into which they had fallen.

Ruinous as the immediate consequences of the downfall of the System were to several individuals, it may, notwithstanding, be said that this project was, upon the whole, rather beneficial than hurtful to France, as the kingdom presently turned more industrious and commercial, the people in general having become better informed with respect to the principles of trade and manufactures. The India Company still subsisting, in a short time equaled, and long continued to rival, those of London and Amsterdam; while different branches of manufacture which had been established by Mr. Law, remained in a flourishing state. It is true that many of the old national creditors were completely ruined by the Mississippi, or at least suffered cruelly in their circumstances; and that several persons had the fate of being raised at once from the depths of poverty to the possession of almost boundless wealth, an elevation that could not fail to superinduce extreme luxury and profligacy, at the same time that numbers were thereby led to neglect their business, and to entertain vain imaginations of making fortunes in the stocks. Some instances of these freaks of fortune have been already adduced, to which we may add, that Madame de la Chaumont,[93]

93. Madame de la Chaumont having been detected in illicit practices against the revenue, was drawn out of the scrape by the exertions of one of the contractors for supplying the French army with provisions. This acceptable piece of service led her to support their interest with so much

a physician's widow, who dealt in millinery at Namur, gained, as some say, to the extent of sixty millions of livres; the Sieur Andre made as much; one M. de Verrue acquired twenty-eight millions; Fargez, once a common soldier in the garrison at Maubeuge, made a fortune of twenty millions; and Messrs, le Blanc and de la Faye eighteen millions of livres each, in the Mississippi.[94]

On the other hand, however, it may be mentioned that several representatives of the most ancient and illustrious families in the kingdom were, by means of the profits they made during the continuance of the System, restored to their pristine glory and splendour. Of this last description the Duc de Bourbon[95] was by far the most successful; and with his gains purchased a vast extent of landed property, rebuilt Chantilly with regal magnificence, established a menagerie there incomparably better stocked than that belonging to his Majesty, and at one

---

warmth, that she soon found herself engaged for them in the sum of 1,400,000 livres, advanced by herself, and borrowed from her relations and neighbours. Coming to Paris to solicit payment, she was forced to accept of that sum in *billets d'état*, although they were then at sixty percent discount. Unwilling to return to Namur with less than would satisfy her creditors, and resolving to risk every thing to accomplish that object, she laid out the whole in the purchase of shares of the India Company immediately on its institution, which happened just at that period, and consequently became enriched beyond her utmost expectations. Hist. Syst. ii. 94.

94. Hist. Syst. ii. 122. Massillon, 107. Mem. Reg. iii. 115.

95. The Duc de Bourbon one day vaunting of the number of actions of the India Company belonging to him, Turmenies, the Royal Treasurer, his familiar friend, took the liberty of saying, 'My Lord, two actions per- formed by your brave ancestor were worth them all;' alluding to the gallant behaviour of the Prince of Conde in two engagements. Duclos, ii. 115.

time imported from England, at a prodigious expense, no less than 150 of the best racehorses he could procure. The Duc de la Force also was exceedingly fortunate; but having made purchases of immense quantities of goods and merchandises, such as spiceries, porcelain, etc. a long and curious process was instituted, to determine whether he had not thus virtually become a merchant, and consequently forfeited the right to his peerage.[96] The Prince of Deux Ponts, the Ducs de Guiche, d'Antin, de Louvigni, d'Etrees, and the Prince de Rohan, were eminently favoured by fortune; and with these may be classed Joseph Gage, brother of the first Viscount Gage. This gentleman (styled by the French writers Monsieur Guaiche,) profited so prodigiously, that he offered three millions sterling to Augustus King of Poland to resign that crown in his favour; and on the refusal of that Monarch to accede to these terms, entered into a negotiation for the purchase of the sovereignty of the island of

96. A circumstantial account of this process may be seen in the Mémoires de la Régence, iii. 82 105, Histoire de France par Fantin, i. 323-333, Histoire du Système, iv. 102, in which last is a satirical print, representing the duke in the character of a porter, loaded with a prodigious burden of all kinds of merchandise, and this punning inscription, *Admirez la Force.* A genealogical history of that nobleman's family is inserted in the *Dictionnaire de Moreri*, under the word Force; and in the perusal of that article one cannot but remark the uncommon longevity of several individuals thereof. James Nompar de Caumont, Duc de la Force, Peer and Marshal of France, died in 1652, in the ninety-seventh year of his age, leaving two sons, Armand Nompar de Caumont, Duc de la Force, Peer and Marshal of France, who died 16th December 1675, aged ninety-five, without surviving issue; and Henry Nompar de Caumont, Duc de la Force, who died in January 1678, aged ninety-five. This last-mentioned nobleman had several children, of whom Jaqueline died 10th May 1702, aged ninety-one, Armand died 16th May 1701, aged eighty- six, and Charlotte died in the eighty-second year of her age.

Sardinia; but the treaty did not take effect.[97]

The System having attracted the attention of all Europe, imitations thereof were quickly attempted by other nations, particularly by Holland and England, among which the famous South Sea Bubble made the most conspicuous figure; but the comparison between this and the Mississippi will not hold throughout, the former having been from the beginning an iniquitous design to enrich a few at the expense of the multitude, by raising the stock through underhand measures, and suffering it to fall again when that end was answered. Mr. Law's System, on the contrary, appears to have been founded on a real intention to extend the commerce and improve the credit of the kingdom; the price of its stock rose in consequence of an infatuation that could scarcely have been foreseen, and it was overturned by an unexampled instance of folly, by which none could have been benefited, and many were ruined.

Having thus brought to a final conclusion the history of this great affair, which, with more point than truth, Voltaire styles 'that astonishing game of chance, played by an unknown foreigner against a whole nation,' it is now time to return to its author, Mr. Law. Appearing in the responsible situation of Comptroller General of the Finances, on the publication of the fatal edict of the 21st May 1720, he could not fail to experience the principal share of the popular indignation, and indeed all the former idolatry of the Parisians for him was now converted into detestation and abhorrence. To appease them in some measure, he, on the 29th of May, went to the Palais Royal to resign his office of Comptroller into the hands

97. Hyst. Syst. i. 33. Voltaire, iii. 12. Lodge's Peerage of Ireland, v. 220. Pope touches upon Mr. Gage's offer in his Epistle to Lord Bathurst on the use of riches:

The crown of Poland, venal twice an age,
To just three millions stinted modest Gage.

of the regent; and his Highness appointed two companies of the Swiss Guards, commanded by M. de Buzenval, to attend his motions, on the pretext of hindering him from leaving the kingdom, but in reality to protect him the more effectually from the fury of the populace. Thus all attempts on his life being guarded against, the people were constrained to give vent to their indignation only in satirical prints and in lampoons, in which *fils ainé de Satan, parpaillot*, and the like names were unsparingly bestowed on him. The Duc de Bourbon thereupon judged it advisable to remove Lady Catherine Law and her family to his seat of St. Maur, fearing further outrages from the tumultuous disposition of the Parisians, rendered frantic by their losses and their poverty to such a degree, as to occasion many to lay violent hands upon themselves.[98]

Nothing remarkable happened to Mr. Law till the 17th July, when the unfortunate affair at the Bank, where many were crushed to death in the crowd, excited such a ferment among the people, that they repaired in vast numbers to the Palais Royal, filling all the courts of that building, and bringing along with them three of the bodies of those who had lost their lives on this occasion. Mr. Law was just going to step into his carriage, after having had an audience of the regent, but at the alarm returned into the Palais, and lay in the Marchioness de Nancre's apartments, where he remained till the 25th July. As his coach was driving off, the coachman had the imprudence to say, they were a parcel of blackguards that deserved to be hanged. This enraged the people so much that they broke the carriage in pieces, the driver hardly escaping with life, while several of the mob were much hurt in the tumult. They now began to be clamorous for Mr. Law to be delivered up to them, but were appeased by the prudent conduct of M. le Blanc, Secretary at War, who, coming out to the gate, harangued the multitude

98. Fragm. ii. 289. Mem. Reg. iii. 5.

in a firm tone, and calling some of the most forward, desired them to carry the dead bodies to the church of St. Eustache, promising a good reward for that service. He then engaged to lay the complaints of the people before the regent; but told them that before this could be done it was necessary they should disperse; which advice the mob, finding their leaders gone, and observing a strong party of troops ready to fall upon them, thought proper to follow without doing further mischief. The first President of the parliament of Paris happening on that day to step out of the assembly, was at the door informed of the disaster that had befallen Mr. Law's carriage; a circumstance that gave him so much joy, as to occasion his scampering back into the court in a manner unbecoming the dignity of his station, crying out,

Messieurs, Messieurs, bonne nouvelle,
Le carrosse de Laws est en cannelle.

The parliament having at this meeting refused to register an edict of the King's Council confirming the commercial privileges of the India Company, and having behaved in a refractory manner on former occasions, it was determined to send the members into exile, in order to get quit of the embarrassments their opposition gave rise to. Accordingly, a corps of mousquetaires, supported by a detachment of no less than 4000 soldiers, were, on the 21st July 1720, sent to conduct the whole members of the parliament of Paris to Pontoise, where they remained in exile till the middle of December following.[99]

---

99. Fragm. ii. 185. Duclos, ii. 116. Richelieu, iii. 225. The opposition of the parliament to the System was, it is said, owing to a proposal made by Mr. Law to the regent, of repaying in bank notes the sums paid by the members of that court for their places, which were in future to be

On the 27th of August following, Mr. Law was, by the King in Council, appointed Director General of the Bank and of the India Company, and Judge Reporter of the Affairs of the Committee of Council established by edict of the same date. He now took up his constant residence in the Palais Royal, where he had assigned to him the apartments formerly occupied by the Marquis d'Etampes, the repairs of which cost the regent 20,000 crowns. Still, however, the Parisians were so much enraged against him, that their rancour burst out on every occasion; and his very name was sufficient to excite tumults, as appears from a circumstance that about this time occurred. One M. de Boursel passing in his carriage along the Rue St. Antoine, had his way impeded by a hackney coachman, whom his servants fell upon, and he got out to assist them. The man cunningly cried out, 'There is Mr. Law who is going to murder me; fall upon and kill him;' a crowd instantly assembled, and with sticks and stones pursued De Bourse into the Jesuits church, as far as the altar; near which observing a little door open, he escaped through it, barring it behind him, to the interior of the convent, but his equipage fell a sacrifice to the fury of the mob.[100]

From this and several other instances, Mr. Law could not but observe how strongly the current of popular indignation

filled by persons holding commission revocable at pleasure. This proposal having been divulged, the parliament were so much irritated, as to resolve to send a party to seize Mr. Law, bring him before them, try him on the spot, sentence him to death, and put that sentence into immediate execution in the court of the Palais Royal. So little, however, did rancour take place in Mr. Law's disposition, that he ever after said they were the best patriots he knew, for choosing rather to forfeit their patrimony and to go into exile, than to register an edict they thought hurtful to their country, and inimical to the general principles of liberty. Duclos, i. 375, ii. 39. Richelieu, iii. 41.

100. Fragm. ii. 290. Examen, i. 334. Mem. Reg. iii 36.

ran against him; and as the month of December approached, his situation became still more dangerous and alarming. The plague, which then raged at Marseilles, at the same time that it increased the discredit of the paper, and the confusion of affairs, augmented the number of his enemies, all the evils befalling the kingdom being absurdly attributed to him. The parliament of Paris, whose rancour against him was confirmed and heightened by exile, were to be recalled in a few days, and he could expect no mercy if once they got him into their clutches; so that he now began to entertain the most serious apprehensions for his personal safety, more especially as the regent had positively refused to permit him to leave the kingdom. He however solicited a license to retire to one of his country seats, in hopes that matters might thus be more speedily composed; and this request being granted, he resigned all his offices. At his last interview with the Duc d'Orléans, it is reported that Mr. Law said, 'My Lord, I acknowledge that I have committed great faults; I did so because I am but a man, and all men are liable to err; but I declare to your R. H. that none of them proceeded from knavery, and that nothing of that kind will be found in the whole course of my conduct.' The regent assured him of his regard and protection; and with these friendly assurances Mr. Law quitted Paris, 'so late his happy seat,' and the theatre of his glory, but now the scene of his disgrace, on the 10th of December 1720, retiring to Guermande, a fine house belonging to him, six leagues from that capital. Two or three days after he had left Paris, the Duc de Bourbon wrote him a kind letter, mentioning that the regent had ordered passports, permitting him to leave the kingdom, to be expedited, and offering to supply him with any sum he required to defray his travelling expenses. This last offer Mr. Law resolved to decline, as a few days preceding his departure from Paris, one of his clerks had brought him 800 louis d'or, received at the mint, in payment of a note for that sum, payable in coin, found among the papers belonging to him, in the possession of the treasurer of the bank; a most acceptable and well-timed supply, as he had not then ten pistoles in specie.[101]

Immediately on receiving this letter, Mr. Law made preparations for his journey; and the next day Messrs, de Lassay and de la Faye arrived at Guermande with the passports, and a large sum of money in gold from the Duc de Bourbon, which Mr. Law, for the reason already stated, declined receiving. The duke also sent with them his favourite Madame de Prie's postchaise, the servants attending it having dark coloured surtouts over their liveries, in order to prevent discovery. In this carriage, Mr. Law and his son set forward to Brussels, attended by four equerries and six horse guards belonging to the duke, having relays provided at every stage. The governor of Valenciennes, (M. d'Argenson, intendant of Maubeuge,) recognising the fugitive, stopped him, on account of the passport bearing a fictitious name. He thereupon produced another passport in his true name; this augmented the perplexity of the governor, who, however, insisted on detaining Mr. Law; but the ex-minister producing a letter from the regent to the Duc de Bourbon, covering these different passports, and granting permission to himself to quit the kingdom, was allowed to proceed on his journey to Brussels. From thence he sent back Madame de Prie's carriage, with a very polite letter of thanks, enclosing a diamond of great value. Lady Catherine Law remaining at Paris under the protection of the Duc de Vendôme, did not leave France till she had discharged all the debts owing by her husband to tradesmen and the like, among which was one of 10,000 livres to a rotisseur.[102]

When the Council of State met on the 16th of December,

101. Fragm. ii. 296. Oeuvres de Law, 425.

102. Hist. Syst. iv. 85. Duclos, ii. 134. Richelieu, ii. 134.

a warm altercation ensued between the regent and the Duc de Bourbon, on the subject of Mr. Law's departure from France. The duke said that Mr. Law had always acted in exact conformity to the orders of the regent, otherwise he would not have granted permission for him to quit the kingdom. The regent accused the duke of giving Mr. Law the passports; that is true, answered the other, but then it was you that sent them to me; I never asked for them, but you directed me to carry them to him. You wished to have him out of France. I am willing to explain the whole affair to the king and council. I never advised that Mr. Law should leave the kingdom, but I opposed the sending of him to the Bastile, and delivering him up to the parliament. We could not have said or done any thing against him which would not have recoiled upon our own heads. You gave me the passports without my asking for them, and charged me to carry them to him, consequently none can attribute to me his departure from France. But, at least, said the regent, did I send your carriage or your guards to escort him? You were then much more interested in his safety than myself; I permitted him to leave the kingdom, merely because I was apprehensive that his presence would impede the cure of the disorders affecting the state, and obstruct the new regulations adopted by government.[103]

Very opposite opinions were entertained as to the effects the departure of Mr. Law would produce. Some complained that the nation was thereby deprived of the assistance of the only person capable of unravelling the entangled thread of affairs, reckoning that all was lost, and looking upon the retreat of Mr. Law as a proof that no more good was expected; while others, on the contrary, rejoiced that the kingdom was no longer given up to the projects of a rapacious foreigner, which, they thought, would in time have occasioned its total ruin. The

103. Richelieu, iii. 193. Duclos, ii. 134.

basest calumnies were spread to irritate the people against the ex-minister; it being commonly reported that several carriages loaded with specie had preceded him to Brussels, in order to enable him to conclude a purchase of some of the provinces of the Low Countries. It was also positively affirmed that he had lodged twenty millions sterling in the bank of England, and large sums in those of Amsterdam, Rome, and Venice, reports that had not the smallest foundation in truth.[104]

It appears that soon afterwards the whole of Mr. Law's property, and that of his brother William, Director General of the India Company, (who was imprisoned in the Bastile,) were seized upon and confiscated. Even a government annuity of 200,000 livres on the lives of Mr. and Lady Catherine Law and their children, for which five millions of livres had been paid, was annulled; although in the edict upon which the annuities had been constituted, there was a particular clause, by which the king engaged they should never be liable to be seized upon or attached for any cause whatsoever, even on his Majesty's account. This was done under pretext that the two brothers were owing twenty millions of livres to the India Company; the falsehood of this assertion was, however, manifested in a memorial sent to the Duc de Bourbon some time afterwards, proving that so far from being debtors thereto, the balance was some millions in their favour. Notwithstanding this fact was clearly established, they found all endeavours to procure restitution of their property unavailing, no part thereof being ever restored to them; a proceeding irreconcilable with justice and common honesty, and which can be accounted for only by referring to the despotic nature of the French government. In consequence, the Comptroller General beheld himself, by the ignorance, obstinacy, and injustice of others, brought down from the height of power and wealth, to a comparatively indigent and

104. Mem. Reg. iii. 73, 74.

abject situation; exhibiting a sad, but not uncommon, example of the insecurity of property, in a state where the will of the executive is paramount to law.

The losses sustained, and the distresses endured by many individuals, in consequence of the failure of the Mississippi System, and the distracted situation of affairs for a long period subsequent thereto, also contributed, in a great degree, to irritate the minds of the people against Mr. Law. However innocent he might have been of having had any hand in advising that fatal edict, it was enough for the parties injured that he was the author of the System; and the ministry were careful not to discourage these sentiments, in hopes of diverting the storm from their own heads. These prejudices, propagated from father to son, are the occasion that even at present numbers hold the name of Law in abhorrence, and do not fail to seize every opportunity to vent their spite against that great minister, whom they look upon as the cause of the calamities their families endured. A remarkable instance of this disposition occurred when Burke's *Reflections upon the Revolution* were translated into French. The latter part of the following passage in that work, 'It is not true that Law built solely on a speculation concerning the Mississippi; he added the East India trade, he added the African trade, he added the farms of all the farmed revenue of France; all these unquestionably could not support the structure which the public enthusiasm, not he, chose to build upon these bases,' was rendered, 'Toutes ces choses reunis n'etoient certainement pas capables de supporter la structure enorme que Penthousiasme du public, et luy, proposerent d'elever sur ces bases;' a complete perversion of the sense, which could not have arisen from ignorance, the translator (M. Suleau, who fell a sacrifice to the fury of the mob at Paris, on the 10th of August 1792,) being skilled in both languages. The Revolution, however, by promoting a spirit of free inquiry, in some measure removed the erroneous notions entertained of the System, to which the Constituent Assembly of France gave a kind of indirect approbation, when they established assignats, these notes being founded on principles similar to those proposed in the first plan for the restoration of credit, transmitted by Mr. Law to the regent.

To the circumstance already stated, as well as to the liberty generally taken with the unfortunate, it is perhaps in a great measure owing, that several of the French writers who have had occasion to treat of the history of these times, have used the freedom of grossly calumniating the reputation of this great man, stigmatizing him as an unprincipled knave, and attributing the downfall of the System to his machinations. The absurdity of this last accusation is evident; and with respect to the charge of knavery, a very strong proof of the uprightness of his intentions arises from the circumstance of vesting his whole acquisitions in landed property in France, not remitting any part thereof to foreign countries,[105] which could have been done with the utmost facility, and obliging his immediate connections, particularly his brother William, and his confidential secretary Robert Neilson,[106] to follow the same

105. Mr. Law sent over orders to his agent in Scotland to purchase for him the estate of Errol in Perthshire; but as he did not remit the purchase money, the bargain was never completed.

106. This Robert Neilson, (son of William Neilson, provost of Edinburgh in 1719,) was bred a merchant in that city, but going abroad, became private secretary to Mr. Law, and one of the principal proprietors of the India Company of France. By the rapid rise of their stock, he was at one time estimated to be worth £150,000 and, at this period, commissioned a friend in Scotland to purchase for him the greatest landed estate on sale in that kingdom. But having been prohibited from remitting any part of his property out of France, he found himself involved in the ruin of his patron, and reduced to beggary. Instead of abandoning himself

honourable line of conduct. The amount of Mr. Law's fortune at the conclusion of the System will afford another refutation of the charge; the following enumeration of his purchases in France being stated on the authority of his nephew, M. Law de Lauriston:

	Livres
Le Marquisat d'Effiat (en Auvergne)	800,000
La Terre de la Rivière	900,000
Le Marquisat de Toucy	160,000
La Terre de la Marche	120,000
La Terre de Roissy	650,000
La Terre d'Orcher	400,000
Terre et Bois de Brean	160,000
Marquisats de Charleville et Bacqueville	330,000
La Terre de Berville	200,000
La Terre de Fontaine Rome	130,000
La Terre de Serville	110,000
La Terre d'Yville	200,000
La Terre de Gerponville	220,000
La Terre de Tancarville (en Normandie)	320,000
La Terre de Guermande	160,000
Hotel Mazarin, et Emplacemens Rue Vivienne	1,200,000
Emplacemens Rue de Varenne	110,000
Emplacemens de la Place Louis le Grand	250,000

to despair, as many in a similar predicament would have done, he travelled into Holland, and there attended to the art of bleaching linen. Returning to his native country a master of that art, he settled at Roslin, where he set on foot the first bleachfield established in Scotland. At this place he resided many years, assiduously attending to his business, and maintaining a most respectable character, after having firmly sustained a change of fortune that the strongest head could scarcely have been able to stand unmoved.

Partie du fief de la Grange Batelière	150,000
Marais ou Chantiers du Fauxbourg St. Honore	160,000
Maisons, surtout dans Paris	700,000
Les Domains de Bourget	90,000
Quelques petites terres, comme Valançay, St. Suplice, etc.	350,000

	7,870,000

Besides the above, it is said that he acquired Lislebonne from the Marchioness de Beuveron, at the price of 500,000 livres, as also Little Rambouillet for 180,000 livres, made offer of 1,700,000 livres to the Duc de Sully for the Marquisate of Rosny, purchased the valuable library of the Abbé Bignon at the price of 180,000 livres, and bought, for 150,000 livres, the place of Secrétaire du Roy, for the sake of the privileges of nobility attached to that office. But the making of these purchases was reckoned a piece of policy necessary for the support of his own credit, and of that of the India Company; and so strict a connection subsisted between these, that it was remarked on disposing of part of his landed property, people began to speak in very dubious terms of his circumstances, and the price of shares suffered a depression. It will also be observed that the aggregate amount of his purchases did not exceed ten millions of livres, a very moderate sum compared with the acquisitions made by several of the adventurers in the Mississippi, Some having realized upwards of twenty millions from nothing; while Mr. Law, the contriver of that project, who brought with him into France above £110,000 sterling, who was at the head of affairs, in the secret of every operation, and disposed of all things at his pleasure, did not make half that sum. His profits can easily be accounted for, when we consider the large share he had in that lucrative concern the General Bank, and the rise in the price of actions of the India Company, although it would appear that he disposed of very few of the shares he possessed therein, as, when he left Paris, he had on their books no less than 4992 actions, which could easily have been sold, when the System was at its height, for upwards of £2,000,000 sterling.[107]

It may, besides, be asked what profit Mr. Law could have possibly made by the decree of reduction, since he was then in possession of as many, if not a greater number of bank notes and actions as any individual in the kingdom. If to these considerations we add the active part he took to prevent the alteration in the style of the notes, and recollect that the whole operations of the System were conducted publicly, the fabrication of bank notes, the creation of shares, and every grant and alienation made to the India Company being done in virtue of public edicts, it appears nothing better than heaping cruelty upon injustice to asperse the character of Mr. Law. The injustice of this conduct is aggravated by its ingratitude, since, if he had not been overruled by the regent and his counsellors, and if the operations of the System had been conducted agreeably

107. It would seem that Mr. Law originally possessed 10,500 shares of the India Company. Of these he voluntarily gave up 2000 to the Company in October 1720; 3000 were deposited in security of a debt of £96,000 sterling due from him to the Earl of Londonderry, Governor Harrison, and other gentlemen; and 300 were assigned for the liquidation of an unjust claim against him to be hereafter noticed. The deficiency of eight shares of the remaining 5000 appears to have been owing to the following circumstance. Soon after his elevation to the office of Comptroller General he made his appearance in the Rue Quincampoix; during the confusion occasioned by the crowd pressing to see him, and crying out Vive le Roi et Monsieur Law, a lady had her pocket picked of near 100,000 livres in notes. On being informed thereof, Mr. Law generously presented her with shares to the amount of what she had lost. Mem. Reg. iii. 66. Hist. Syst. iii. 8.

to his advice, France was in a fair way of becoming one of the richest and most flourishing states in Europe. Whatever love he might once have felt for his native country, he had completely transferred his affections to France; of which, when he was prime minister, his constant discourse was, that he would raise the nation so high that every kingdom in the world should send ambassadors to Paris, while his most Christian Majesty would only dispatch couriers to the other courts in return.[108]

Mr. Law arrived at Brussels in the morning of the 22nd December 1720, passing under the name of M. du Jardin; but as soon as it was known who he really was. General Wrangel the governor, the Marquis de Pancallier, and several of the principal persons in that city, went to pay their respects to him. He waited on the Marquis de Prie the same afternoon at five o'clock, and afterwards accompanied Madame de Pancallier to the theatre, where a vast concourse of people were assembled to behold so extraordinary a character. Next day, the 23rd, the Marquis de Prie returning Mr. Law's visit in great state, brought him home in his coach to a most sumptuous entertainment, at which were present several persons of the highest quality. That evening Mr. Law went again to the play, and, after it was over, supped with the Marquis d'Esquillache. On the 24th he dined a second time with the Marquis de Prie, to whom having notified his intention of leaving Brussels the same evening, that nobleman ordered passports to be got ready; and Mr. Law accordingly set out at nine at night, accompanied by his son.[109]

He came to Venice early in January 1721, still passing under the name of M. du Jardin, and continued in that city two months, partaking of all the pleasures the Carnival afforded, and living on terms of intimacy with the Imperial and French ambassadors. The famous Cardinal Alberoni, the Spanish

108. Lord Stair's Letter of 23rd September 1719.

109. Historical Register, ad ann. 1721.

minister, coming there in February, had an interview with Mr. Law; and it was reported that the Chevalier de St. George also arrived *in cognito*, and had a conference with these ministers in the Capuchin monastery. Whether this last particular was true or not, cannot now be certainly known; only it seems that at this period the Chevalier was not seen publicly at Rome for several days, and when he appeared again he looked so well, that little credit was given to the report that had been circulated of his indisposition. In the mean time, the most extraordinary stories were told of Mr. Law, tending to impress people with an idea of his being possessed of immense wealth. It was said that 160,000 pistoles had been lodged on his account in the bank of the Holy Ghost at Rome, by some persons unknown; that he had offered a vast sum to be admitted into the order of Venetian nobility; and that his son was to be married to a daughter of the Duc de Cesarini, who had a fortune of 100,000 crowns; and that he had drawn bills of exchange to the extent of 250,000 pistoles.[110]

While such reports were spread, Mr. Law found himself under the necessity, in order to secure himself against the claims of pretended creditors, of having his name enrolled in the list of Roman citizens, it being one of the privileges of that body to be exempted from arrests and prosecutions for debt, at the suit of any other than a fellow burgher. Having taken this necessary precaution, he left Venice, on the 15th of March, for Ferrara, on his way to Rome; but receiving intelligence that some of his creditors had assigned their debts to a Roman citizen, who had concerted measures to have him arrested immediately on his arrival, he judged it advisable to return to Venice. After some stay there, he travelled through Bohemia and Germany to Hanover, where he had the honour of an audience of Prince Frederick, and then proceeded to Copenhagen. During his

110. *Ibid.*

residence at this place, having received an invitation from the British ministry to return to his native country, he embarked on board the Baltic squadron, commanded by Sir John Norris, being accommodated in that admiral's own ship. Landing at the Nore on the 20th of October 1721, he proceeded to London, was presented to King George I by Sir John, and took a house in Conduit Street, where he was daily visited by numbers of persons of the first quality and distinction.[111]

The favourable manner in which Mr. Law was received, occasioned no small umbrage to the anti-ministerial party, and was judged of importance sufficient to occupy the attention of Parliament. For when the House of Lords met on the 26th of October, Earl Coningsby represented to that august assembly how dangerous it might be, on several accounts, to entertain and countenance such a man as Mr. Law, and desired that a day might be appointed for taking this matter into consideration. Their Lordships having appointed the 9th of November for the discussion of this business, Earl Coningsby on that day resumed his argument, saying, that, for his part, he could not but entertain great jealousy of a person who had done so much mischief in a neighbouring kingdom, and who, being so immensely rich as he was reported to be, might do a great deal more hurt here, by tampering with many who were grown desperate by being involved in the calamity occasioned by the fatal imitation of his pernicious projects; that this person was the more dangerous, in that he had renounced, not only his natural affection to his country, and his allegiance to his lawful sovereign, by being naturalized in France, and openly countenancing the Pretender's friends; but, which was worst of all, and weighed most with him, that he had also renounced his God by turning Roman Catholic; concluding, that their Lordships ought to inquire whether Sir John Norris had orders

111. *Ibid.*

to bring him over. To this last part of the earl's speech. Lord Carteret answered in substance, that Mr. Law had, many years ago, the misfortune to kill a gentleman in a duel; but that, having received the benefit of the king's clemency, and the appeal lodged by the relations of the deceased being taken off,[112] he was come over to plead his Majesty's most gracious pardon; that there was no law to keep an Englishman out of his own country; and as Mr. Law was a subject of Great Britain, it was not even in the king's power to hinder him from coming home if he thought fit. To this Lord Trevor replied, that Mr, Law was indeed a subject of Great Britain, and, therefore, as such, had an undoubted right to come into the kingdom; but that the circumstance of a person of his character being brought on board of an English admiral, and at this juncture, might deserve the consideration of the House. Earl Cowper spoke much to the same effect; but the matter was suffered to drop; and Mr. Law, on the 28th of November following, pleaded, at the bar of the King's Bench, his Majesty's pardon for the murder of Mr. Edward Wilson in 1694, being attended, on this occasion, by the Duke of Argyll, the Earl of Ilay, and several other friends.[113]

Among the letters to and from the Countess of Suffolk, is one from Mr. Law to her, then Mrs. Howard, dated Tuesday, of this tenor: 'Can you not prevail on the Duke to help me something more than the half year? Or is there nobody that could have good nature enough to lend me one thousand pounds? I beg that, if nothing of this can be done, that it may only be betwixt us two, as I take you as my great friend; and I am very well

112. 'Having found means to pacify the surviving relations of Mr. Wilson, by the payment, it is said, of no less than £100,000.' Nichols's Leicestershire, iii. 487. The magnitude of the sum renders the accuracy of the anecdote doubtful.

113. Parliamentary Register.

assured of it by the honour I had done me yesterday at court by the king. I had another letter yesterday from France, with the same thing over again. Excuse this, dear madam, and only put yourself in my place, and know, at the same time, that you are the only friend I have. Yours, etc. LAW.'[114]

The editor of these letters observes thereon, 'This melancholy avowal that Mrs. Howard was his only friend, affords a striking instance of the instability of fortune, power, and friendship. This letter was probably written in the winter of 1721. The following passage will describe what the writer had been in the beginning of 1720. Our projector had arrived at an unexampled pitch of wealth and power. He possessed the ear of the regent, he was almost adored by the people, and was constantly surrounded by princes, dukes, and prelates, who courted his friendship, and seemed ambitious of his patronage. Such was the immensity of his wealth, that he bought no less than fourteen estates with titles annexed to them; among which was the Marquisate of Rosny, which had belonged to the great Duke of Sully, the friend and minister of Henry IV Yet within two years he could find no one good natured enough to lend him £1000, and had no friend but Mrs. Howard, who was probably not three months acquainted with him.

In 1721 he arrived in England, where he was at first treated with much distinction, and, it would seem from this letter, had some kind of pension or allowance.'[115]

After this, Mr. Law continued to reside some years in England. He had received intelligence of the confiscation of his

---

114. The Countess of Suffolk was nearly connected with Lady Catherine Law, whose grandmother, Elizabeth. Countess of Banbury, was sister of Theophilus Earl of Suffolk, grandfather of her husband, Charles Earl of Suffolk. 'The Duke was probably John Duke of Argyll, head of the Campbells, Mr. Law's maternal ancestors.

115. Suffolk Letters, i. 87.

whole property in France; but being conscious of the rectitude of his conduct in the management of the finances, and that the balance would, upon examination, be found considerably in his favour, he had good reason to flatter himself with the hopes of recovering a large sum, especially as the regent always professed a more than ordinary regard for him, and continued punctually to remit his official salary of 20,000 livres per annum. He carried on a constant correspondence with that Prince, who at last came to acknowledge, that he had no doubt but the System would have succeeded, if unexpected events had not obliged him to deviate from the plan originally laid down. His Royal Highness manifested his approbation of Mr. Law's conduct, confessed that he still stood in need of his instructions, requested his opinion upon the then state of affairs, and concluded with saying, that his only dependence for bringing France to its true value was upon his abilities and knowledge. Under these impressions, the regent had several consultations with the council upon the propriety of recalling Mr. Law, which he had set his heart on doing.[116]

In these proceedings the British ministry took no small interest. Sir Robert Walpole wrote to Sir Luke Schaub: 'Whitehall, 10th April 1723. Your letter of the 22nd instant, N. S. is just come to hand, and I am very glad that the conduct of his Majesty's ministers at Hanover meets so much with the approbation of the Duke of Orléans. This correspondence is above all things to be cultivated; and I have always read with pleasure the several accounts you have sent me of the good disposition of the Duke of Orléans. It would be a great misfortune if his uncertain temper should expose him to the influence and directions of persons less well affected to the king's interest than the present ministers of France give us great reason to hope they are; and I know not what is certainly to be

116. Massillon, 199.

determined with that view in regard to Mr. Law. If the Duke of Orléans is disposed to recal him, as Mr. Law's friends here are very sanguine in hoping, it is not our business to obstruct it. But it is not easy to judge what is most to be wished for in this case, unless we know the competition, and upon whom the favour and confidence of the Duke of Orléans might probably fall. If Mr. Law does not return, there can be no doubt but that the power might fall into worse hands; and if any who are neither Englishmen by birth or affection should prevail, we should have a less chance than by admitting one who has sundry ties to wish well to his native country. But, perhaps, Mr. Law's being thought agreeable or acceptable in England would not at all forward his return to France; for nothing but his being thought not only an able but a good Frenchman can secure his being recalled.'

Sir Robert Walpole thus expresses himself in a letter to Lord Townshend: 'Whitehall, October 12, 1723. I have seen Mr. Law several times since I had your directions how to behave to him, and have shewn him all reasonable civilities; and I am sure I have so ordered my brother's journey to Paris with him, that he thinks Horace goes with his advice, and has not the least suspicion of any such thing being ordered from Hanover. He was very pressing with me that Horace should go that way, and thought it would be of great use and satisfaction to the Duke of Orléans to talk with one so nearly related.'[117]

It does not appear whether Mr. Law then went to Paris. The regent died suddenly on the 2nd of December 1723, which was a fatal blow to Mr. Law. His expectations of recovering part at least of his property now became fainter, his pension ceased to be remitted, his embarrassments increased, prosecutions were commenced against him both in France and England,

117. Coxe's Life of Sir Robert Walpole, ii. 252, 274. 'Horace' was Sir Robert's brother Horatio, first Lord Walpole of Wolterton.

and he was threatened with imprisonment by some of his creditors, from which, however, he was relieved by two noble lords becoming his sureties. His distresses are feelingly detailed in a letter to the Duc de Bourbon, Prime Minister of France after the decease of the regent, dated at London, the 25th of August 1724. In it he says, that 'there is scarcely an example, perhaps not one instance, of a stranger like him who acquired, in so high a degree, the confidence of the Prince, who made so large a fortune in so upright a manner, and who, on leaving France, reserved nothing for himself and family, not even what he had brought into the kingdom with him.' This letter was accompanied with a memorial, stating his situation previous to being employed in the finances, his conduct during his administration, and his condition at the date of the epistle.[118]

These papers were followed by a long memorial, dated at London, 15th of October 1724, wherein Mr. Law examines at length the demands made upon him by the India Company, and proposes a mode of liquidating them. The demands upon him appear to have been as follows:

		Livres	*s.*	*d.*
1.	Balance of a former account, comprehending the sum of 2,521,000 livres of subscriptions for shares, remitted by the Sieur Bille to Mr. Law, to be paid in by his clerks	4,072,514	2	3
2.	Issued by edict of the 23rd May 1721, for the support of families brought from Germany, and sent to Louisiana by Mr. Law	450,000	0	0
3.	Tin and lead furnished by the Company to Mr. Law	32,639	17	0

118. Oeuvres de Law, 398.

4. Paid by the Company in Genoese money to M. de Chavigny	275,184	17	4
5. Bank notes delivered to Mr. Law, 29th November and 15th December 1720	7,437,342	0	0
6. Receipt of one of the clerks of the Company in the department of *Primes**	4,500,000	0	0
7. Paid by the Company to Mr. Law's correspondents	4,468,694	16	0
	20,236,375	12	7

*See below[119] for an explanation of Primes.

Mr. Law readily acknowledges, that he ought to be held bound to pay the first article in shares; although he at the same time observes, that in the former account therein referred to, there was stated the sum of five millions of livres laid out in the purchase of annuities upon his own life, and the lives of his

119. Primes, or first payments, were sums advanced upon engagements to furnish shares of the India Company, at a fixed price, within a stipulated period, as was commonly done by those who could not readily procure actions. The traffic in Primes increased to such a height, that it was found necessary to issue an edict, dated 11th of February 1720, prohibiting all bargains of that sort between individuals, the Company engaging at the same time to deliver, within a stated period, shares to those who applied for them, and paid down a certain proportion of the price by way of advance. These, also called Primes, were, by a subsequent edict, directed to be brought back to the Company, the holders getting in return one share for each 9000 livres of Primes so brought back. Dict. de Moreri, au mot Actions. Hist. Syst. iii.

wife and children, seized upon by the king, as formerly noticed The second article he does not dispute, supposing the sum in question to have been issued for the support of some hundreds of families brought, at his own expense, from Germany, in order to be sent to Louisiana, to assist in the cultivation of that province, who were waiting for embarkation at Port l'Orient at the period of his dismissal. The third article he also allows, the tin and lead having been provided for the service of the navy, and he having charged the amount among the sums advanced by him for his Majesty. The money paid to M. de Chavigny he likewise allows; as also the fifth article, which, he says, was employed, by special order of the regent, in purchasing, at a high price, actions from persons whose cases appeared uncommonly favourable. As for the receipt of the clerk, the subject of the sixth article of the claim, he absolutely denies that he is debtor to the Company on that head, and asserts no demand could be more unjust and ill founded, the receipt running in these terms: 'I grant myself to have received from my Lord the Comptroller General, the sum of 4,500,000 livres to account of ten millions of Primes, which I have delivered to him. Paris, 13th February 1720,' signed by the clerk. Now, this receipt does not prove that Mr. Law owed 4,500,000 livres; bearing only that he had paid that sum to account of ten millions; so that if he had not made a second payment, he would have been owing 5,500,000 livres on that score. The clerk did not pretend to say that he had delivered the ten millions of Primes to Mr. Law, without obtaining, at the same time, a receipt from him for that sum; but no such receipt was produced. Mr. Law therefore says that the fact will be found to be precisely this, that on paying the balance of 5,500,000 livres due from him for the Primes, he had given along with it the receipt of the clerk for 4,500,000 livres. Notwithstanding the injustice of thus bringing him in debtor for the last-mentioned sum, upon the authority of a receipt which, so far from proving that he was owing, bore on the face thereof that he had paid it, Mr. Law readily agreed that the company might, if they pleased, deduct that sum from the amount of his shares, as, in owing four or five millions less to them his situation would not be bettered, the property in their hands belonging to him being double or treble the amount of their demands, and it was his wish to get back only what he had brought with him into France. As to the seventh and last article, he acknowledges that the company was entitled to require payment thereof in specie from his brother William, but asserts that the king was the real debtor for the sum in question, it having been employed, by orders of the regent, in the payment of subsidies.

After stating that, on the evening before he set out for Guermande, he had remitted to Pomier de St. Leger, two millions in bank accounts, worth at that time 700 percent, or fourteen millions, in order to discharge what he was owing to the India Company, but that Pomier had thought proper to disobey his directions, he proposes the following mode of liquidating the before-mentioned demands:

		Livres	*s.*	*d.*
1.	Bank accounts	7,475,640	4	7
2.	500 shares, at 9000 livres each, to discharge the receipt in the department of *Primes*, converted into shares at the rate fixed by edict of council	4,500,000	0	0
3.	Effects belonging to him in possession of the King and India Company, as per particular list	4,792,040	12	0

4. Warrants on the Royal Treasury, for payment of the subsidies and other articles advanced by Mr. Law for the King's service	3,468,694	16	0
	20,236,375	12	7

He therefore beseeches the Duc de Bourbon that his Highness would be pleased to expedite warrants from the king for the above 3,468,694 livres, 16s. as also for 2,159,957 livres, 17s. 6d. owing by his Majesty on the same account, proposing, with this last sum, to discharge the demands of his foreign correspondents.

After doing so, he stated that there would remain due to him 5,389,906 livres, 3s. 9d. in effects in the possession of the king and India Company, besides 4492 actions carried to the *Visa* by the Sieur Nicolas; and he left entirely to the duke to settle these claims in whatever manner his Highness thought proper, at the same time hinting that his wishes were limited to the recovery of the money he had brought with him into France in 1714, amounting to 1,600,000 livres, at twenty-eight livres to the marc, or somewhat more than £114,000 sterling.[120]

In the conclusion, Mr. Law mentions that he did not include in the state of his debts £96,000 sterling due from him to the Earl of Londonderry, Governor Harrison, and others, since 3000 shares of the India Company were assigned for payment

120. At the death of Louis XIV the standard of the silver coin being 28 livres to the marc, each livre was worth 17 and one-half pence. The standard was frequently altered during the Regency of the Duc d'Orléans, and the subsequent administrations of Louis XV being sometimes rated at 80 livres to the marc and under, or less than 6d. each livre, a circumstance which prevented the conversion, with precision, of the sums of French money mentioned in this work to sterling.

of that sum. He earnestly entreated the duke to order these shares to be settled in such a manner as to liquidate the demands of these creditors, and to free him from his engagements to them; but this reasonable request met with no attention from government, although the shares in question were, at the period of the assignation, valued at upwards of one million sterling. Some passages selected from this memorial paint the situation of Mr. Law and his family in strong colours. 'When I retired to Guermande, I had no hopes that the regent would have permitted me to leave the kingdom; I had given over all thoughts thereof, when your Highness sent to inform me of his intention to accord that permission, and the next day, immediately on receiving the passports, I set off. Consider, my Lord, if, being in the country, removed from my papers and books, it was in my power to put in order affairs that required not only leisure, but also my presence in Paris, to arrange properly; and if it is not a piece of great injustice for the India Company to wish to take advantage of the condition to which I was reduced, and of the dishonest conduct of clerks, in requiring from me payment of sums I do not in fact owe, and which, even though I had been owing, were, as I have shewn, expended for their service, and payable in actions or notes, of which effects belonging to me they at that time had, and still have, on their books to the amount of double or treble the sum they demand. No, my Lord, I cannot bring myself to accuse the company of so much as the intention to injure me. That company owes its birth to me. For them I have sacrificed every thing, even my property and my credit, being now bankrupt, not only in France, but also in all other countries. For them I have sacrificed the interests of my children, whom I tenderly love, and who are deserving of all my affection; these children, courted by the most considerable families in France, are now destitute of fortune and of establishments. I had it in my power to have settled my daughter in marriage in the first houses of Italy, Germany, and England; but I refused all offers of that nature, thinking it inconsistent with my duty to, and my affection for, the state in whose service I had the honour to be engaged. I do not assume to myself any merit from this conduct, and I never so much as spoke upon the subject to the regent. But I cannot help observing, that this mode of behaviour is diametrically opposite to the idea my enemies wish to impress to me; and surely all Europe ought to have a good opinion of my disinterestedness, and of the condition to which I am reduced, since I no longer receive any proposals of marriage for my children.

My Lord, I conducted myself with a still greater degree of delicacy, for I took care not to have my son or my daughter married even in France, although I had the most splendid and advantageous offers of that kind. I did not choose that any part of my protection should be owing to alliances, but that it should depend solely upon the intrinsic merits of my project.'[121]

Every argument, however, that Mr. Law could urge to procure restitution was of no avail, the company persisting to demand payment in specie of the sums owing them, and refusing to allow him credit for the notes and actions in their hands belonging to him, while government declined to account for his real and personal property in France, confiscated and sold by them. He was therefore constrained to renounce all hopes of favour or justice from that quarter. It does not appear how he settled his affairs in Britain. Sir Robert Walpole, in a letter to Lord Townshend, 29th July - 9th August 1725, says, 'Mr. Law has wrote to your Lordship, to desire that he may have some sort of commission from his Majesty to any prince

121. The late M. Law de Lauriston, nephew of the Comptroller General, transmitted to the author a complete copy of this memorial, which has never yet appeared in print. Some detached fragments only are published in the Oeuvres de J. Law, Paris, 1790, 8vo.

or state, not to be made use of, but to be kept as a protection in case of necessity. By what he says to me 1 really believe it may be of service to him, and I promised to use my interest with your Lordship for the obtaining it.'[122] It is probable that this request, thus supported by the Prime Minister, was complied with; and it appears that Mr. Law finally quitted Britain the same year, 1725, and fixed his residence at Venice.[123] The famous President Montesquieu happening to pass through that city some time afterwards, did not omit to pay his respects to so extraordinary a person, and frequently visited Mr. Law. One day the conversation chancing to fall on the opposition made by the parliament of Paris to the System, Montesquieu could not help asking how it happened that he had not endeavoured to gain over that body by bribery, as, he said, Sir Robert Walpole had proceeded with respect to the British senate. In answer, Mr. Law desired the president to remark the wide difference between these two bodies: Le sénat Anglois ne fait consister la liberté qu'à faire tout ce qu'il veut. Le François ne met la sienne qu'à faire tout ce qu'il doit. Ainsi l'intéret peut engager l'un à vouloir ce qu'il ne doit pas faire, il est rare qu'il porte 1'autre à faire ce qu'il ne doit pas vouloir.[124]

At Venice Mr. Law concluded the chequered course of his life, dying there in a state but little removed from indigence, on the 21st of March 1729, in the fifty-eighth year of his age; and he lies buried in one of the churches of that city, where

122. Coxe's Life of Sir Robert Walpole, ii. 473.

123. It is said that when Mr. Law's funds were reduced to £1000, he publicly offered, in one of the cities of Italy, to stake the same against a shilling, that double sixes would not be thrown six times running. The number who adventured was so great, that Mr. Law soon doubled his capital, and the magistrates found it necessary to prohibit this gambling.

124. Nouvelle Dictionnaire Historique, au mot Law.

a monument to his memory is still to be seen. The following epitaph appeared soon afterwards:

Ci git cet Ecossois célèbre,
Ce calculateur sans égal, Qui, par les regies de l'algèbre,
A mis la France à l'hopital.[125]

His external appearance, as has already been mentioned, was uncommonly engaging, very few being reckoned his equal in personal graces; and his conversation, enlivened with wit, and seasoned with repartees, was no less attractive. Uniting to these qualifications distinguished politeness, and the most agreeable and insinuating manners, he hardly ever failed to conciliate the regard of those who came near him.[126] The Duchess Dowager of Orléans relates, that considering he was a foreigner, he did not speak the French language ill; and her Royal Highness highly commends his polite, yet spirited, behaviour on first coming into power, an instance of which will be found in the subjoined note.[127]

125. Mercure d'Avril 1729, p. 814. Nouv. Diet. Hist, ubi supra.

126. Law étoit d'un tattle haute et bien proportionnée; il avoit l'air grand et prévenant, le visage ovale, le front élevé, les yeux bien fendus, le regard doux, le nez aquilin, et la boucbe agréable; on peut, sans flatterie, le mettre au rang des homines les mieux faits. Son esprit répondoit à son exterieur. Tout cela joint à ces manieres douces et insinuantes, lui attiroit l'estime et la confidence de ceux qui l'approchoient. Hist. Syst. i. 69. Grand, bien fait, d'un figure agréable et noble, de beaucoup d'esprit, d'une politesse distinguée, avec de la hauteur sans insolence. II y avoit chez lui plus d'ordre et de proprete que de luxe. Duclos, ii. 134.

127. M. Laws a eu violent querelle avec ce fou De (the Prince of Conti) qui vouloit lui forcer à faire une chose expressement défendu par mon fils. Sçavez vous bien que je suis, demanda-t il à Laws? Oui, répondit celuici, sans cela je ne vous respecterois pas comme je fais. Vous devez done

In Bromley's Catalogue of British Portraits, four engravings or designs of Mr. Law are noticed: (i) folio, engraved by l'Anglois; (ii) quarto, designed by Hubert; (iii) quarto, engraved by Des Rochers; and, (iv) quarto, painted by Rigand, and engraved by F. de Schmidt. In the Earl of Orford's gallery at Strawberry Hill was a portrait, in crayons, of 'John Law, Inventor of the Mississippi Scheme, and Prime Minister to the Regent Duke of Orléans, one of the best of Rosalba's works.'[128] His Lordship wrote to a friend: 'Strawberry Hill, 14th November 1792. I have a portrait of Law, and should not object to letting a copy of it be taken, but I doubt that could not be done. Being in crayons by Rosalba under a glass, and any shaking being very prejudicial to crayons, I fixed the picture in one of the niches of my gallery, under a network of carving, whence it cannot possibly be removed without pulling the niche to pieces. The picture, too, being placed over the famous statue of the eagle, there is no getting near to it, and I certainly could not venture to let a ladder be set against the eagle. Indeed, as there are extant at least three portraits of Law, there does not seem to be another wanting. I am sorry I cannot give you a more satisfactory answer about Lady Wallingford. I have met her at two or three places, but I did not visit her, nor have I the least knowledge of her husband's family, nor can I direct you at all where to inquire. I did not even know that there is an Earl of Banbury living.'

The superiority of Mr. Law's talents is best evinced by the circumstance of his raising himself, by them alone, to the first place in point of power and consequence, in a nation accustomed to regard all foreigners, especially his countrymen, in a very inferior light; while the Mississippi System, a project perfectly

m'obéir, dit l'un. Je vous obéirai, dit l'autre, quand vous serez Régent. Fragm. ii. 271.

128. Orford's Works, ii. 463.

original in its nature, and interesting from the number, the variety, and the importance of the objects it comprehended, furnishes a strong proof of the extent of his genius, the greatness of his views, and the fertility of his resources in the execution of his plans.

To his moral character no compliments can be paid. His uncommon personal endowments generally insured him success in affairs of gallantry, and to these unworthy pursuits he devoted too much of his time. Lockhart of Carnwath relates, that, even before he left Scotland, he was 'nicely expert in all manner of debaucheries.' It is said that he lived several years in a course of adultery with an English lady, whom he had persuaded to elope from her husband, and to accompany him in his rambles abroad; and the Duc de Richelieu speaks in very plain terms of the attachment the Duchess Dowager of Orléans had for Mr. Law.[129] The excess to which he carried the destructive vice of gambling has been already noticed.

Besides the works already mentioned, *Proposals and Reasons for Constituting a Council of Trade*, and *Money and Trade Considered*, each of which has gone through two editions, Mr. Law published in France some tracts upon Credit and Finance. Towards the end of 1790, there appeared at Paris an octavo volume, entitled, *OEuvres de J. Law, Controleur General des Finances de France sous le Regent*. This volume, published by M. Senouer, captain of engineers, contains, first, Mr. Law's classical work, *Money and Trade Considered*, translated into French. Secondly, two memorials on the subject of banks and banking, presented by Mr. Law to the regent. Thirdly, Fifteen letters on

129. La Duchesse Douairière vivoit publiquement avec Law. Mémoires de Richelieu, ii. 180. Law, un des plus beaux hommes de son terns, se chargea de lui (la mère du Régent) faire la cour et de lui plaire; et la Princesse s'en accoramoda; car dans son vieux age elle avoit encore le témperament des jeunes demoiselles de vingt ans. iii. 11.

the same subject, addressed to that Prince. And, fourthly, a letter, with some extracts from a memorial, sent to the Duc de Bourbon from London in 1724, formerly noticed. This book, enriched by the intelligent editor with a preliminary discourse, and illustrated by valuable notes, is in high estimation in France, and has contributed not a little to remove the erroneous opinions of the System entertained in that country.

Mr. Law married Lady Catherine Knollys, third daughter of Nicholas third Earl of Banbury, by his second wife Anne, daughter of William Lord Sherard. Lady Catherine, who was first married to a gentleman of the name of Senor, by whom it does not appear she had any issue, was born 1669, and died 1747, according to the following pedigree, communicated by the late Earl of Banbury:

Thomas Boleyn, Earl of Wiltshire and Ormond

- Lady Anne Boleyn, married to King Henry VIII
  - Elizabeth I, Queen of England
- Lady Mary Boleyn, married to William Carey
  - Catherine Carey, Sir Francis Knollys, K.G.
    - William Earl of Banbury
      - Nicholas Earl of Banbury
        - Lady Catherine Knollys

By Mr. Law she had one son, John Law of Lauriston, and one daughter, Mary Catherine, a very accomplished lady, who, during the height of the Mississippi System, had the most splendid and advantageous offers of marriage from the first houses of England, France, Germany, and Italy. She espoused, 4th July 1734, her first cousin, William Viscount Wallingford, major in the first troop of Horse Guards, eldest son of Charles fourth Earl of Banbury, by his first wife, Margaret, daughter of Edward Lister of Burwell, in Lincolnshire. His Lordship, who was born in 1690, was elected Member of Parliament for the borough of Banbury, on a vacancy 1733, re-chosen at the general election 1734, and continued to represent that place till his death, 6th June 1740, aged fifty, when a patent was making out to call him to the House of Peers, by the style and title of Baron of Althorp, in the county of Lincoln, (where he had an estate,) which his sudden demise prevented from taking effect. By his death the family sustained an irreparable loss, particularly his widow, who was at that time dangerously ill with smallpox. Leaving no issue, his half-brother, the Rev. Charles Knollys, became Viscount Wallingford, and afterwards fifth Earl of Banbury, on his father's decease at Dunkirk, 26th August 1740, in the seventy-ninth year of his age. Lady Wallingford, surviving her husband more than half a century, died at her house in Park Street, Grosvenor Square, London, 14th October 1790, leaving her nephew and cousin, Thomas Woods, seventh Earl of Banbury, her executor and residuary legatee.[130]

John Law of Lauriston, only son of the Comptroller General, did not fail, during his father's prosperity, to have his full share of the adulation and courtship lavishly bestowed on his family. He was frequently in the company of the young King, Louis XV and had the honour of being named, along with some noblemen of the highest quality, to take a part with his Majesty in a superb ballet, planned by the Maréchal de Villeroi; but he was prevented from enjoying that honour by an attack of the measles. His education was entrusted to Charles Chesneau,

130. Communications from the late Earl of Banbury.

Sieur du Marsais, an able, disinterested, and benevolent character, whose eulogy is prefixed to the seventh volume of the Encyclopédic. In May 1720, the Duc de la Force being appointed ambassador to London, in order to arrange several matters of importance with the British ministry, Mr. Law resolved to accompany his grace, and had actually taken his departure from Paris with the duke's brother and other young noblemen; but obstacles arising, a courier was dispatched with orders for them to come back. After the downfall of the System, Mr. Law resided chiefly at Chantilly and St. Maur with the Duc de Bourbon, and in December 1720 accompanied his father in his retreat from France and subsequent travels. He afterwards settled with his mother at Utrecht and Brussels, succeeded his father in 1729, and died a cornet of the regiment of Nassau Friesland, of the smallpox, at Maastricht, in February 1734, aged about thirty-one, unmarried. After his death, the widow St. Paul of Paris made a demand on Lady Catherine Law of the sum of 200,000 livres, due to her in consequence of a transaction during the Mississippi System with young Mr. Law, then only seventeen years of age. The claim being resisted, a process was instituted to compel payment, and several letters that passed on the occasion between the then Duke of Portland and Lady Wallingford are in the archives of the Banbury family.[131]

John Law of Lauriston thus dying unmarried in 1734, the succession to the estate of Lauriston fell to be regulated by the settlements executed by his grandmother, Jean Campbell. By entail dated 7th April 1703, Lauriston was devised to John Law, her eldest son, and the heirs male of his body, which failing, to William, Robert, and Hugh Law, her third, fourth, and fifth sons, and the heirs male of their bodies respectively, which failing, to her own heirs and assignees whatsoever. By a deed

131. Duclos, ii. 73. Fragm. ii. 271. Mem. Reg. ii. 401. Communications from the late Earl of Banbury.

dated 18th July 1707, she ratified the former entail in so far as concerned her said four sons, and the heirs male of their bodies, which failing, to the heirs female of John her eldest son, and failing these, she ordered Lauriston to be sold, and the purchase money to be divided as therein directed. Of course William Law, her third surviving son, succeeded to the estate of Lauriston, on the extinction of the issue male of the Comptroller General.

The subjoined notices of the family of Law of Lauriston may not be uninteresting. William Law, the first of Lauriston, and his wife Jean Campbell, had eleven children:

1. Agnes, born 1st February 1666, married in 1685 to John Hamilton, writer to the signet, only son of James Hamilton, minister of Eagleshame, second son of James Hamilton of Barncleuth, and had issue.132

2. James, born 19th December 1667, died in infancy.

3. Jean, born 12th September 1669, married to John Hay of Letham, M. D. grand-nephew of Sir John Nisbet of Dirleton, and had one daughter.

4. John Law of Lauriston.

5. William, born 14th September 1672, died an infant.

6. Andrew, born 22nd November 1673, a goldsmith or banker in Edinburgh, who was passed over in the entail. He married, 27th January 1695, Bethia, daughter of John Melville of Murdocairney in Fife, a cadet of the family of the Earls of Leven and Melville, by whom he had a son Alexander, born 22nd February 1697, who died an infant, and a daughter Jane, married to Walter Brebner, writer in Largo, and had three daughters, Lilias, married to David Goodsir, Law, married to John Dempster, and Bethia, married to James Grundiston

After the death of their grand-uncle, William Law of Lauriston, in 1752, these three ladies took the legal course

132. Douglas' Peerage, i. 203.

for getting themselves served his nearest and legitimate heirs portioners of entail, of the reformed religion. This being opposed by John Law of Lauriston, eldest son of William, the Court of Session, in 1756, repelled the reasons proponed against the service, and allowed it to proceed; and this decision was, on appeal, affirmed by the House of Lords, 7th February 1757.133 They did not, however, succeed in getting possession of the estate of Lauriston. Their descendants are heirs of line of the Comptroller General.

7. William Law of Lauriston, born 24th October 1675.

8. Janet, born 9th September 1677.

9. Robert, born 6th October 1678.

10. Lilias, born 19th October 1680, married, first, in 1698, to James Clerk; secondly, to James Martin.

11. Hugh, born 10th January 1682.[134]

William Law of Lauriston, the third surviving son, born at Edinburgh, 24th October 1675, was settled in London, whence he was called to Paris to assist in the operations of the Mississippi System, was Director General of the India Company, and one of the Directors of the Royal Bank of France. Succeeding to Lauriston in 1734, he was served heir of his brother John, 1st July 1747, and had a charter, under the great seal, of the lands of Lauriston, on the 27th of the same month, to himself in liferent, and in fee to his eldest son and the heirs male of his body, with other remainders. He died at Paris in 1752, in the 77th year of his age, leaving by his wife, Rebecca Dives, four daughters, of whom one married, first, M. de la Cour, secondly, M. le Comte de Bermondet; another married M. de Boisseroles, the other two died unmarried; and two sons, John Law of Lauriston, his

133. Morison's Decisions, 9612. Appeal Cases.

134. Wood's Ancient and Modern State of the Parish of Cramond, 162, where it is stated that Robert and Hugh died unmarried; but no evidence has been received to that effect.

successor, and James Francis Law, born 1724, who, after much active service in India, died in 1767, in the forty-third year of his age, at the Isle of France, on his voyage to Pondichery, in quality of Commander-in- Chief of the troops of the French East India Company. He married Miss Carvalho of Madras, of the Portuguese family of Pombal, by whom he had one son, James Francis Law, born 1758, an officer in the French army, (who married, and has issue;) and three daughters, the eldest married to M. de Bruno, the third to Samuel Johnson, Esq. one of the Council at Madras, and the second, F. Xavier Charlotte, second wife of Charles Smith, Esq. Governor of Madras, is mother of Culling Charles Smith, Esq. married, 9th August 1799, to Lady Anne Wellesley, sister of the Marquis of Wellesley and Duke of Wellington, relict of the Hon. Henry Fitzroy.

John Law of Lauriston, the eldest son, born 19th October 1719, after very important services in a civil and military capacity in India, detailed in the Ancient and Modern State of the Parish of Cramond, 251-263, rose to the rank of Marshal de Camp, Governor of Pondichery, Commandant General and President of Council of all the French settlements in India. He succeeded to the estate of Lauriston on the death of his father in 1752, and died at Paris about 1796, having married, in 1755, Miss Jean Carvalho, daughter of a Portuguese gentleman settled at Calcutta, by whom he had nine children:

1. Jean, born 8th March 1757, married, in 1777, to the Comte de la Fare Lopez.

2. Anne, born 21st December 1761, died 2nd December 1762.

3. John, born 31st July 1765, died 19th December following.

4. John William Law de Lauriston, born 8th September 1766, an accomplished officer of the French navy, who embarked on board the Astrolabe frigate, commanded by his

friend the Vicomte de l'Angle, in the unfortunate expedition of discovery under M. de la Perouse, of which no tidings have been received since the ships composing it visited Botany Bay in February 1788.

5. James Alexander Bernard Law de Lauriston, born 1st February 1768, the representative in the male line of the Comptroller General, a nobleman of the highest consideration in the French court, and a Peer of France under the title of Count Lauriston. On the 6th of June 1823 he was raised to the dignity of Marshal of France, in room of the Prince of Eckmuhl deceased, and appointed Commander-in-Chief of the second corps of reserve of the French army in Spain.

6. Charles Louis, born 11th July 1769.

7. Joseph Charles, born 20th August 1770, died unmarried.

8. Francis John William Law, born 2nd August 1771, a merchant in London. On the 21st May 1808, he was served nearest and legitimate heir of entail and provision, of the reformed religion, of his father John Law, and entered into possession of the estate of Lauriston, to the exclusion of his elder brothers, who are Roman Catholics.

9. Louis George, born 6th August 1773.[135]

The descent of the Laws of Lauriston from James Law, Archbishop of Glasgow, and the Laws of Bruntoun, in Fife, is stated[136] on the authority of the late Walter Scott, Esq. writer to the signet, father of the most celebrated, interesting, and delightful author of the present day. Mr. Scott was agent for the late Marshal de Camp Law of Lauriston, and communicated a distinct account of that family, which, coming from an able and accurate professional gentleman, may be considered as authentic. A different account of the descent of the family

135. Wood's State of Cramond, 264.

136. See page 3.

is given by Nisbet[137] under the article, Roberton of Earnock: 'Bartholomew Roberton, on the 17th October 1608, is contracted to Margaret Law, daughter lawful of John Law of Waterfoot, in Mearns,' (a parish of Renfrewshire;) 'she was sister to Mr. Andrew Law, minister of Neilston, grandfather to John Law, Esq. the great Mr. Law, who was General Governor of the Finances of France.' A manuscript account of the family of Robert Wodrow, author of the History of the Sufferings of the Church of Scotland, written by him about 1720, contains the following paragraph: 'For about seven years he,' (Mr. Wodrow, the author's father,) 'had now a safe recess at Eagleshame, from the terrible barbarity of the times. It is a very retired corner; and he not only enjoyed the comfort of his relations, but the advantage of the gospel by, and conversation with, Mr. James Hamilton, indulged there to his death, about the end of the year 1684, and the benefits of a grammar school for his children, and those of several friends who came and lodged with him in his house, taught by Mr. Michael Rob, who was the first Presbyterian minister ordained after the liberty, at least in the west. I mind, among his scholars, there was one about the year 1683 or 1684, who of late has made a surprising figure and blaze throughout all Europe, John Law, son to a goldsmith at Edinburgh, whom his father sent to Eagleshame, both to be removed from the temptations of Edinburgh, and to be under the care of Mr. Hamilton, who was nearly allied to him, and to be under my father's inspection, who was pretty nearly related to him by his mother, and the Dunlops of Pulnoon Mill, one of whose sisters, if I remember right, was married to Mr. Law, minister of Neilstoun, grandfather to this Mr. Law.'[138]

137. Heraldry, ii. Appendix, p. 156,

138. Communicated by Mr. George Robertson, Bower Lodge, Irvine, author of several well-known publications, who compiled an account of Mr. Wodrow the historian, still in manuscript, principally from that

This residence of Mr. Law at Eagleshame probably led to the matrimonial connection of Mr. Hamilton's only son with his eldest sister, which took place in 1685.

The arms of Law of Lauriston are thus blazoned. Ermine, a bend between two cocks, gules. Crest, a unicorn's head proper. Motto, *Nec obscura nec ima*.

book, which is in the possession of Miss Wodrow at Saltcoats, grand-daughter of the historian.

THE LIFE OF JOHN LAW

APPENDIX

THE LIFE OF JOHN LAW

APPENDIX

The following translation from the *Cours d'Economie Politique* of M. Henri Storch, vol. iv. p. 130, Paris, 1823, affords such a clear and succinct view of the Mississippi System, that it has been judged proper to subjoin it by way of Appendix; although the author does not appear to have correctly estimated the character of Mr. Law, and represents his motives and intentions in a very unfavourable light.

In the course of the eighteenth century France has been twice the victim of paper money; first, under the Regency of the Duke of Orléans, by the famous System of Law, and again by the assignats during the Revolution.

The history of the System of Law embraces such a variety of facts, and these facts so complicated, that it is difficult to find a clue to conduct us out of the labyrinth. But as it is of less importance to follow the historical detail of the System, than to mark its spirit and consequences, I shall confine myself to the events which are important in this view, passing by the others however curious in themselves.

France, at the death of Louis XIV found herself burdened

with a debt of 3111 millions of livres tournois, bearing an interest of eighty-six millions. There was no means of meeting this debt but by the excess of revenue over the ordinary expenditure, which, in time of peace, amounted only to nine millions. The regent named a commission called the *Visa*, which, by the most arbitrary operations, reduced the debt to 2000 millions, and the interest to eighty; yet the government was just as unable to discharge the reduced, as it had before been to discharge the unreduced debt.

At this crisis Law, a Scotchman by birth, presented to the regent a project for relieving the state from this load of debt by means of credit, and without injuring the interest of individuals. Before entering on the details of this project and of its execution, it will be necessary to develop the principles of its author respecting the nature and effects of credit. This analysis will be the more useful, as the ideas of Law on this subject are still extensively adopted in Europe.

Money, said Law, is only the sign which represents riches in circulation. Gold, silver, copper, leather, notes, shells, and every other material used to estimate or measure real riches, are only riches of confidence or opinion which form what is called credit. A louis d'or, a crown, are notes, of which the impress of the prince is the signature: and as things are only valuable according to the purposes that they serve in society, it is indifferent whether a louis, a note for the same sum, or even shells, are employed to represent the value of other commodities.

It is unnecessary to refute this sophism. Law ranked in the same class metallic money, and fictitious or conventional money; but there is this difference between them, that the one has an intrinsic value and the other not. The first is not a mere sign but real wealth; the other, on the contrary, is only a sign. Metallic money has scarcely need of confidence or credit to preserve its value, whilst fictitious money only exists by credit; that is to say, by the persuasion that it can at any time be exchanged either for coin or other commodities. Without doubt things only receive their value from their usefulness; but metallic money has a double use, it may either be employed as money, or as a useful and precious metal; whereas fictitious money can only be employed as counters.

Besides, gold and silver can only be obtained by long and painful labour, or at a very considerable expense of production. The material of fictitious money, on the contrary, scarcely requires any labour, and, consequently, its quantity may be augmented at pleasure. In fine, the value of gold and silver is more invariable than that of any other commodity, while that of paper fluctuates with every change of popular opinion. It is not indifferent, then, as Law assumes, whether one use a louis or a note to represent the value of articles. Law, having established for the basis of his System the principle we are now examining, found himself dragged into the most absurd consequences. 'In a country,' said he, 'where there exists no circulating medium but gold and silver, its riches may be greatly augmented by the introduction of paper money.' This consequence, true to a certain extent, he admitted in an indefinite sense. Paper money augments the national riches only by filling up the place of the metallic currency, which is disengaged from its employment as money, to serve other purposes, or to be exchanged for other riches. Law, on the contrary, imagined that the metallic currency, with the additional paper money, would continue to circulate together as money. He did not perceive that there might be too much circulating medium in a country; that this superabundance causes the specie to leave it; and that the paper, increased beyond the demands of circulation, would sink in value. He thought that the increase of the circulating medium would have no other effect than to lower the rate of interest, and that it would be absorbed by the increase of industry; and thus the abundance of paper money appeared to him only an additional source of public prosperity. But the rate of interest does not in any degree depend on the quantity of the circulating medium; and abundance of money encourages industry, inasmuch only as it is convertible into capital.

In a state, said Law, where the people are not accustomed to credit, (as was the case in France at the epoch of the System,) it is enough to double the amount of the circulating medium, by adding to the specie an equal value in notes; credit ought not to exceed the amount of specie, that notes may always be convertible into cash at the pleasure of the holders. He was not aware, that doubling the amount of the currency by an issue of paper money will not double the value of the money in the country, and that such a measure would only have the effect of banishing the specie from circulation. But let us suppose for a moment that gold and silver should circulate along with the paper, and that specie should not be depreciated, it by no means follows that the notes would be always convertible into cash at the will of the holders.

The specie into which they are to be convertible is not in the possession of the prince, nor of the bank that issues the notes, but of the public; and will the individual possessors of cash consent that their money shall serve as a guarantee for the credit of the bank, and be employed when necessary to pay its notes? Certainly not. Credit can never be founded on such a basis. The money belonging to the individuals of a nation can never be held as security for the notes which a sovereign or a bank may choose to issue. If this security is not to be found in the treasures or resources of the prince, or in the coffers of the bank, it is a mere illusion.

Such a credit, however, said Law, would be rather a multiplication of specie than credit; for, according to his doctrine, credit consists in the excess of notes over specie, and the advantage to be obtained is only in this excess. The absurdity of this doctrine is too palpable to require much time to expose it. Law considered the whole nation as one grand banking company, and his reasoning was nearly this: If a bank may increase the issue of its notes beyond the amount of its funds in bullion, without risking its solvency, a nation may do the same. On these principles he proposed to establish a bank, into which was to be transferred all the metallic currency of the nation, which was to be replaced by bank notes. This project, gigantic and chimerical as it was, did not appear so to Law or the regent: they believed the execution of the thing possible, and they attempted it.

In 1716 Law laid the foundation of his famous System, by the establishment of a bank for the issue of notes, for which he had obtained an exclusive privilege from government. The funds of this bank were raised by shares, and the notes were payable at sight, in specie of the same weight and fineness as the money in circulation at the period of their issue. This clause alone made them be sought after. Since 1689 the currency had been subject to perpetual alterations: the clause in the bank notes secured the holders against these arbitrary proceedings; and as the bank faithfully kept its promise, the notes were so much preferred, that they bore a premium of one percent above metallic currency. The good conduct of the bank in the issue of its paper, its promptitude in fulfilling its engagements, and the universal want of credit procured for it the greatest confidence, and disposed the nation to regard its founder as a genius capable of reviving the credit and commerce of France, at a period when they were almost annihilated.

The following year, 1717, Law procured for his bank the exclusive privilege of a commercial company, established under Richelieu, called, *La Compagnie d'Occident*, or the West India

Company, which had been long in a languishing state. The bank created 200,000 shares of 500 livres each, payable in state paper, for which the government set apart a perpetual revenue of four percent. This measure absorbed 100 millions of the public funds that were most depreciated; but these funds could not form stock for a commercial enterprise. From the irregular payment of the interest they were depreciated to such a degree, that 500 livres of nominal value in these funds could not be sold for more than 160 or 170 livres; yet the bank took them at the full nominal value. This combination of the operations of banking with commercial speculations was essentially vicious. These two kinds of business are of a nature absolutely incompatible; the chances of commerce may endanger the certainty of the gains of a bank, or at least shake its credit. That which gives confidence in a bank issuing notes, is not exclusively its stock, which is not, and can never be of the same amount as its notes in circulation; but it is the belief that it issues its notes only in exchange for good securities which will insure their payment. When a bank issues notes for commercial speculations, often disastrous, and always precarious, these notes have only an uncertain guarantee, and its credit is just proportioned to this uncertainty.

The public were not aware of the danger to which the bank was exposed by the union of these two undertakings. The French had no accurate ideas respecting the nature and constitution of banks, and were, at the same time, misled by the blind confidence which they placed in Mr. Law. A purely accessory circumstance tended greatly to increase this confidence. The interest of the 100 millions of *billets d'état* which the bank had acquired by the sale of its shares, being more regularly paid to the bank than it had formerly been paid to individuals, the shares which at first had been bought for 160 or 170 livres, soon rose to par, that is, to 500 livres. The advance of the *billets d'état* to a rate so advantageous to the holders, increased the value of those that remained in circulation. This effect, which was solely owing to the regular payment of the interest, was attributed to the operations of Law. The French, astonished at the sudden rise of their depreciated paper, looked on it as a kind of miracle; their delusion became boundless, and from that moment the most puerile confidence outran all the mystifications of this famous political charlatan.

The regent perceiving that bank notes were in demand, and that quantities of specie were daily carried to the bank, it was easy for Law to persuade him that it was quite possible to draw into it the whole of the circulating specie of the kingdom, and to replace it by the same amount of paper money; that by this means almost a half of the public debt of France might be paid off, and that the credit of the bank would be sustained, since it would always be able to pay in specie what notes might be returned to it. In consequence of this extravagant project, the bank was administered on account of the king, from the 1st of January 1719. The regent reimbursed the shareholders, took the establishment into his own hand, and gave it the appellation of the Royal Bank. This was only an apparent change, for Law still continued to direct all its operations. At this period the notes which it had issued amounted to 59 millions.

Till now the notes had been paid at sight; and although they flattered themselves they would be able to continue to pay them in the same manner, even supposing the fullest extension was given to what Law called credit, it was thought prudent, nevertheless, to take the precaution of securing a resource, in case prompt payment should become impossible. For this reason the notes issued by the royal bank did not promise *to pay in specie of the same weight and fineness as the specie then in circulation*, but merely to pay in SILVER COIN. This change, though slight in appearance, was fundamental. The notes previously issued stipulated for a given quantity of silver, of the same fineness as that which circulated at the period of their issue, under the denomination of a livre. The notes that were now issued stipulated only for a certain number of livres, and thus opened a door for all the fluctuations which it might please arbitrary power to occasion in the real value of the coin called a livre. This was called fixing the value of paper money; but in reality it was rendering it changeable, and it did change most deplorably.

In getting the bank declared a royal establishment, Law flattered himself that the public would continue to carry specie to it to be exchanged for notes; but his expectations were disappointed. Whether the tenour of the new notes inspired some distrust, or whether, in fact, the notes already issued were sufficient for the purposes of commerce, the demand for notes ceased, and Law saw himself forced to change his tactics, in order to draw coin to the bank, and to promote the circulation of the notes which he intended to issue to an immense amount.

He concerted with the regent another project to relieve him from the national debt, the most extravagant and criminal stock jobbing project that has ever appeared. Two plans presented themselves to his imagination for sustaining the credit of the notes even under the most extensive issues. The first consisted in insensibly transforming bank notes into a real paper money. For this purpose it was agreed to give a preference to paper over specie, by declaring the value of the one fixed and invariable, whilst, by perpetual alterations, they were to render the other continually fluctuating and uncertain; to exact payment of taxes in bank notes; to introduce them by degrees into all transactions instead of specie; and, at last, entirely to prohibit the use of specie, when the nation should have been completely disgusted with it. The second method was to contrive an outlet for the immense sums of paper which the repayment of the state creditors would throw into circulation, by offering the holders an apparently very lucrative investment for this paper, in order to prevent their coming to the bank to have it exchanged for specie. With this view it was agreed that Law should unite to the West India Company, which was still under his direction, several other commercial and financial undertakings, out of which he should form one colossal establishment, and that he should divide this establishment into shares, of which the amount should be equal to the whole of the public debts. The regent was to buy these shares with the paper money that he was to manufacture; to borrow anew this paper in order to pay the creditors of the state; and then to sell the shares to retire the paper money.

This plan promised more success than the first. The union of a number of lucrative concerns under the direction of one man, whose skill and talents inspired the greatest confidence, would naturally encourage a very high idea of the profits of the company, and make the shares be sought after. The government, in appearing to desire to partake of these advantages, would strengthen this idea; and as the company would make no scruple to accept paper money from government in payment of its shares, this measure would again give credit to the paper money. If this project had succeeded, the state would have been relieved from an immense debt by means of a yearly income perpetually payable to the company; and its creditors, having become shareholders of the Company, would have followed its fate. Thus, the effect of the System was not only to inundate the kingdom with paper money, but likewise to change the creditors of the state, and to transfer them to the company; that is to say, to convert capital that was secure into very hazardous funds, and fixed revenues into what were very precarious.

Having matured this plan, they set themselves about putting it in execution. The East India Company, also established by

Richelieu, was then, like that of the West, at the lowest ebb. In May 1719[139] they were incorporated together under the name of the 'Company of the Indies;' 50,000 new shares were created at 550 livres each, payable in specie, these shares only gave an obligation on the Company's funds for 500 livres, the same as the former, but the public were already so strongly impressed with the enormous profits that the Company would make that they might have been sold a great deal higher. The proceeds of the sale of these 50,000 shares amounted to 27,500,000 livres in specie; a small portion of this was set apart to build ships, and these trifling preparations raised the hopes of the public so high that more shares were eagerly sought after. In consequence of this, 50,000 more were created a month afterwards, and sold at 1000 livres each.

The Government neglected no means of impressing the nation with an idea of the great profits which the Company would make. The Company had undertaken, during the preceding year, to farm the revenue of tobacco; the king likewise made over to it the mint for 50 millions of livres. It likewise contracted for the *fermes générales,* and then engaged to lend the king the immense sum of 1600 millions, at three percent interest, that is to say, for an annual income of 48 millions; in fine, the Company obtained the collection of all the revenues of the State. It then declared to its proprietors that it was in a condition to pay a dividend of 200 livres upon each share. The rate of interest being then at four percent, such a dividend was equal to the interest of a capital of 5000 livres, provided the dividend had been secure and permanent; but as the public had no doubt either of the amount of the dividend, or of its permanence, shares rose to 5000 livres.

The first shareholders, better informed than the others in

---

139. This period was the true commencement of the system, which fell to the ground on the 21st May 1720; it thus existed exactly one year.

regard to the situation of the Company, sought to render their fortunes secure by the sale of a part of their shares, the produce of which they employed in the purchase of landed property and other commodities. The opulence so rapidly acquired by these shareholders was a new cause of seduction to the public; every one hastened to buy shares; a general delirium pervaded the nation; every profession was abandoned for that of stock jobbing; inhabitants of the provinces, strangers, all hastened to Paris to enrich themselves by the purchase of shares. This business, indeed, opened a door to opulence; the stock jobbers continually stimulated the fluctuations in the price of shares, and in skillfully profiting by these fluctuations, even obscure and wretched individuals rapidly rose to the most brilliant fortunes.

The shares being brought by four successive creations to their complete number, that is, to 624,000, the king ordered that the state creditors should be paid off in bank notes. Such immense sums thrown all at once into circulation could not easily find employment except in the purchase of the Company's stock; thus the public creditors paid off found themselves in some measure constrained to employ their capital in this manner. This new competition caused the price of shares to rise to 10,000 livres.

The creditors of the state were thus forced, by the manoeuvres of Law, to buy shares in the Company of the Indies, at the rate of 10,000 livres, if they expected to secure to themselves any income at all. And what did they receive for their 10,000 livres? One share of capital stock valued at 500 livres; their capital was embarked in a hazardous commercial enterprise; it only entitled them to a determinate, but uncertain part of the gains of a newly commenced company, which, of course, must be precarious. Supposing even that the clear revenue of the Company had regularly amounted to 12,480,000 livres, this would only have given 20 livres of annual interest for each share. Indeed the company had promised an annual dividend of 200 livres a share; but granting that the promise had been serious, and the effect practicable, the result still is, that the stockholder who employed 10,000 livres to purchase one share, is made to lose one half of his revenue. But how was it possible that the Company could raise annually 124,800,000 livres for the dividend upon 624,000 shares? This charge was so utterly beyond its strength, that even the apologists of the System must acknowledge the absurdity of its speculations, and the cruelty of its conduct towards the public creditor.

It is evident, then, that the System was only intended to relieve the state from its debts by the ruin of its creditors; the higher the shares rose, the greater was the amount of public debt that each absorbed; and hence it appears that the excessive price to which the shares were carried entered into Law's plan. But the excessively high price of the shares, and the prodigious gain of the original proprietors were, of themselves, sufficient to occasion the fall of the System. It was natural that these lucky speculators should consider by what means they might best realise the gifts of fortune, and this was exactly what happened. The great number of shares sold by the proprietors diminished their price, so that neither the company nor the regent was able to effect further sales. The bank soon felt the effects of this shock: the holders of notes instantly made a run upon it for specie for their notes.

In this crisis Law determined to employ the most violent means to save his system, to replenish the emptied coffers of the bank, and to give a forced currency to the notes. By his advice the Government affected the greatest contempt for specie it permitted, and even ordered it to be sent out of the kingdom it forbade the importation of gold and silver coin. It farther ordered that the bank should receive no more cash to be exchanged for notes that all creditors should be permitted to demand notes from their debtors, even in cases where these last were more valuable than coin that the Company should be held bound to pay the produce of the different imposts under its charge in notes, and that it should be authorised to demand payment in the same notes from the tax contributors; all judicial offers not made in notes were declared void; small notes were introduced; lastly, to degrade the coin, and to wean the nation from the use of it, a new coinage was ordered of very small pieces of little value. The value of notes was legally fixed at five percent above that of specie; and it was forbidden to offer, or receive payment in silver, of any sum exceeding ten livres, or in gold of any sum exceeding 300 livres; while all payments of bills of exchange were to be made in notes. The fluctuations in the value of the coin succeeded each other with inconceivable rapidity; the coin designated by the name of livre was at different times a 28th, a 40th, a 60th, an 80th, a 120th, a 70th, and a 65th part of a marc of fine silver. Law caused these fluctuations in the specie, on purpose to fill the coffers of the bank, which were as quickly emptied by the more prudent of the persons enriched by his System; he encouraged by these means the preference of notes to gold and silver, with the view of entirely interdicting the use of these two metals; a decree to which effect received the sanction of Government on the 27th of February 1720.

By this famous decree it was ordained that no person of whatever condition, and even no religious community, should keep in his or their possession more than 500 livres in specie, under penalty of confiscation of all that should exceed that sum, and a fine of 10,000 livres; it was likewise forbidden, under the same penalties, to any person to retain in their possession any article of gold or silver. The officers of justice were enjoined to visit the houses, communities, privileged places, and even the palaces and royal mansions; and the king declared that the specie or articles seized should be the reward of the informers. In fine, it was prohibited, under a penalty of 3000 livres, to pay a sum of 100 livres or upwards otherwise than in bank notes.

The rigour and novelty of such a law spread alarm through the whole kingdom. Many, under the influence of fear, carried to the bank all the gold and silver they had in their possession; others, and these the greater number, resolved at all hazards to disobey. Nevertheless search was generally made informers were encouraged the servant was dreaded by his master brother suspected brother, and parents were afraid of their own children. Distrust broke the union of families every citizen was on his guard against another and terror was redoubled by frequent condemnations. During an interval of about three weeks the bank received nearly 44,000,000 livres; but their coffers resembled the cask of the Danaids, it was impossible to fill them. At last the decree of the 11th of March 1720, entirely proscribed gold coin, and silver crowns, leaving only the smaller pieces in circulation.

From the 1st of January, 1719, to the 20th of May, 1720, during the short space of 505 days, the bank had issued notes to the immense amount of 2,235,000,000, which were employed in paying off the public creditors. The consequences of this unheard of abuse of paper money did not at first appear, because during the course of the year 1719 the issues had been moderate; but when, during four months of 1720, they manufactured 1,925,000,000, nothing could prevent their fall. Specie having entirely disappeared, the paper money with which the country had been inundated, and which, consequently, was greatly depreciated, only remained in circulation; the price of every thing advanced daily, and in an alarming progression. Government now felt that too great an extension had been given to what Law called credit; it became sensible that to re-establish the value of paper, it would be necessary to diminish its amount; but as Government was neither able nor willing to repurchase the notes, it satisfied itself by reducing their nominal value one-half. The decree of 21st of May, which ordered this reduction, was a deathblow to the whole System. The public perceived at last that paper property was precarious and illusory; the next day every one was anxious to get rid of it at any price.[140]

The regent, seeing the lamentable consequences of the decree, revoked it six days afterwards; he advanced the nominal value of the specie, and re-established that of the notes, but all his measures were useless. The depreciation of the notes was such, that the holders accepted from the Government such proportion of state funds as they were pleased to offer for them,

---

140. As bank notes did not appear to sink in value when compared with specie, the greater number of contemporary authors imagine that their value was not affected up to the 20th of May, and that it would have continued to have been maintained but for the decree of the 21st, which was a death-blow to their credit. This opinion, which is maintained by Stewart, as well as by the French authors, is evidently false; it is impossible that the circulation of a country, whose money before this period was not reckoned to exceed 1,200 millions, could absorb 2,235 millions of paper money, consequently this last must sink in value. The writers on the System, as well as the evidence of experience, prove the truth of this position; all agree in saying that the prodigious quantity of paper money had excessively advanced the price of provisions, and that the nominal value of the notes was only reduced with the view of diminishing these prices; but the high price of all sorts of merchandise is the result of the low value of the money with which they are purchased; if the notes of the system bore a premium over specie, it was only because the Government received them at this rate in payment of taxes, but at bottom this preference was factitious and chimerical. How was it possible to estimate the value of notes by that of specie in a country where specie had been prohibited, and where the bank only paid small notes of ten livres?

at the rate of a 50th and even a 100th part of their nominal value. The ruin of the bank crushed in its fall all the individuals whose interests were connected with it: besides, this bankruptcy lost to the public creditors upwards of 44,000,000 of annual interest, and a capital of more then 844 millions and a half.

If the credit of the bank notes could not be maintained, it is evident that that of the shares of the Company's stock must have sunk still more. Their value had not only not been declared legally fixed, nor had the king guaranteed them as he had done the bank notes; but their dividends, uncertain in their very nature, depended on the success of a tottering company, which had embarked in operations too vast and too dangerous to realise great or solid profits; thus the fall of the Company's stock was still greater and more rapid than that of its notes.

What pen can describe the confusion and ruin of France on the retreat of Law? Gold and silver had been hidden or exported to foreign countries; Dutot himself acknowledges that 500 millions, at 65 livres the mark, had been carried out of the country; but when the fall of the notes, as of the Company's stock, had become public when 9000 livres in paper were given for a single mark in gold what a vast deal more must have been exported! One of the inferior cashiers of the Company remitted to Holland 20 millions of florins, and quitted the kingdom. All credit, public as well as private, was annihilated; distrust was the greater, as every individual was ignorant of the state of his own fortune; it was only known that the greater number had been ruined, and it was difficult to distinguish the few who had escaped the general shipwreck. The price of commodities was tripled and quadrupled; it was impossible for persons of limited incomes to subsist without encroaching on their capital. It was necessary to augment the pay of the soldiers by one sous per day. Labourers were without employment, manufactures and commerce were at a stand, rents, dividends, wages, and pensions, were no longer paid; a small number wallowed in wealth, whilst poverty overwhelmed the great mass of the community.

The situation of the public finances was not less deplorable, there was not a single sous in the public treasury; the king found himself without revenue, all his resources having been long since drained; thus although the present was horrible, the future appeared still more alarming. Deliverance from the national debt was the only good that the system had accomplished, and this brought along with it the ruin of the creditors and the exhaustion of the whole kingdom.

FINIS.

INDEX

MORE FROM NEWTON PAGE

John Law of Lauriston: Financier and Statesman, Founder of the Bank of France, Originator of the Mississippi Scheme

A. W. Wiston-Glynn

ISBN-13: 9781934619032

The Financier, Law: His Scheme and Times. A Graphic Description of the Origin, Maturity and Wreck of the Mississippi Scheme

André Cochut

ISBN-13: 9781934619049

The Mississippi Bubble: A Memoir of John Law

Adolphe Thiers

ISBN-13: 9781934619056

John Law's Money and Trade Considered: A Hidden Foundation of Modern Economic Thought

Gavin John Adams

ISBN-13: 9781934619094

Letters to John Law

Gavin John Adams

ISBN-13: 9781934619087

Made in the USA
Monee, IL
08 November 2026

67383838R00094